In this book, Mark solves one of the sa prospecting uncertainty in todc environment. This is a practical guide that are buyer-focused, laden with influence and structured in a way that yields results.

To top it all off Mark starts with the pillar of mindset, knowing that the right actions come from a place of heightened awareness.

His simple methodology makes for easy learning, practical application and reinforcement that can be committed to. Want to be a performing SDR or AE with a solid, modern, prospecting foundation that values quality over quantity, then this book is for you.

John Dougan
Head Of Global Sales Delivery & Coaching.
Workday

Mark's book, Tactical Pipeline Growth, provides sales teams and their managers an excellent guide to achieving repeatable sales success through a customer-centric engagement focus..."

Duncan McGregor
Sales Enablement Professional
ASX Top 50 Companies Including
Qantas and Coca-Cola Amatil

This is not another sales book. This is a blueprint and 'how to' action plan for prospecting success. Mark truly understands what it is like to be in the shoes of a modern sales professional and provides a systematic approach to driving consistent and compelling outreach strategy.

I'm going to use these outreach templates for my top 20 clients this quarter.

Oscar Collingwood-Smith,
Ent Account Exec, MindTickle

I have had the good fortune of working with the author Mark McInnes. Everything he teaches in this book he has tested and proven himself. He is a highly successful sales coach and he is sharing ALL his prospecting secrets in this great book. Highly recommended for ANY sales professional (experienced or novice) looking for new insights to engage prospects in today's "socially connected" world.

Joe Micallef
Banking Sales Capability Expert.

For companies trying to re-establish momentum in their business, filling the funnel on a daily basis is not optional.

Mark's book contains many immediately usable tactics to get going in a structured and measurable way, leading to building more high-quality pipeline quickly.

A prospector's handbook, end to end. Plus, he's a fair dinkum guy too!

Phil Cleary
Head of Sales Enablement, Salesforce APAC

"Tactical Pipeline Growth" is one of the most adaptable sales books I have ever read. It can be put in practice chapter by chapter to gain fast results after implementing. His range of examples, templates, scripts and cadence rhythms combine the foundation with relevance to execute the content within a realistic time frame....

Mark published an excellent guide with "Tactical Pipeline Growth" raising the bar for new sales books – especially as more sales conversations are needed than ever.

Gunnar Habitz,
Senior Partner Alliance Manager APAC, HootSuite

To all my brothers and sisters in the sales trenches, if you're looking for some great advice at growing a robust, strong sales funnel, check out "Tactical Pipeline Growth" by Mark McInnes. It's a real winner – Thumbs up from me.

Rob Garland,
Account Manager, Print Specialist.

One of the best reads out there. Written with practical advice given Mark's years of experience and not theoretical wish wash. I really enjoyed this and have my team reading it too. We've embodied many of these principles into our sales playbook.

Michael Savanis
General Manager, ANZ

I've been in sales all my life. The touches and examples in the book are extraordinary.

This should be a subject at tertiary level education. Well done.

Dan Adams
Sales & Marketing Director.

Always be prospecting.

A full pipeline solves a lot of problems.

Best books to help you achieve a steady flow of leads.

1 Fanatical Prospecting by Jeb Blount

2 Combo Prospecting by Tony J. Hughes

3 Predicable Revenue by Jeremy Donovan, Marylou Tyler

Now, we can add "Tactical Pipeline Growth" by Mark McInnes. This is the manual on doing the basics well and consistently to achieve effective new business outreach.

Steve Burton
Head Of Sales (Voted UK best Sales Trainer 2018, 2019)

I highly recommend this book to anyone in business development. Having read dozens of books on sales and sales training, this is a gem.

Most sales books claim all previous books on sales represent 'the old way' of selling and their book is the only book you need from now on. Most books have 400 pages with a few useful insights, but also a lot of fluff.

This book, however, isn't about making bold claims. It is extremely practical, takes under 3hrs to read and leaves you with plenty of tips you can put into practice straight away, as well as templates and scripts for you to make your own.

Will definitely recommend this to all my peers.

Peter Boshuizen
Senior Account Exec, SaaS.

TACTICAL PIPELINE GROWTH

WINNING THE OUTBOUND BATTLE FOR NEW BUSINESS

MARK MCINNES

First published in 2020
www.markmc.co/tpg

First Edition

© Mark McInnes 2020

ISBN: 978-0-646-81993-8

The moral rights of the author have been asserted.

Editing + Proofreading by Cavalletti Communications, www.cavacom.biz
Cover Design and typesetting by Luke Harris,
WorkingType Studio — www.workingtype.com.au

Disclaimer
The material in this publication is of the nature of general comment only, and does not represent professional advice. It is not intended to provide specific guidance for particular circumstances and it should not be relied on as the basis for any decision to take action or not take action on any matter which it covers. Readers should obtain professional advice where appropriate, before making any such decision. To the maximum extent permitted by law, the author and publisher disclaim all responsibility and liability to any person, arising directly or indirectly from any person taking or not taking action based on the information in this publication.

Table of Contents

Foreword

My Kung Fu Si-Gung, Malcolm Sue, would say luck is all about labouring under the correct knowledge.

If you follow the execution strategies Mark has shared in this book, I can promise you all the sales luck you'll need.

I've had the pleasure of executing sales performance projects with the world's largest companies, in over 25 countries for over 20 years. In that time, I've been paid tens of millions of dollars to help them define the difference between their top performers and the rest of their sales reps.

I've come across the promise of making sales, without having to sell, in every country and every industry. But the truth is, this 'promise' is still a marketing pipedream.

There is still no substitute for talking to more of the right people, with the right message at the right time. The good news for all sales reps aspiring to be better is that the difference is not something we are born with or linked to intelligence of any kind. The difference is not adopting the latest research-based sales techniques or having the latest sales technology and tools.

As I've seen in project after project globally, the best tools in the world are useless until someone uses them. I can confidently say, the difference is focus and consistency of effort.

Mark embodies focus and consistency of effort across every aspect of his life.

His ability to do the right work daily has made him an amazing salesman, consultant, husband, athlete, and friend. I've had the pleasure of working with Mark on sales performance projects for over five years.

In that time, I've been constantly amazed at his ability to cut through all the noise, develop simple and smart new business campaigns, and then doggedly execute them on a daily basis for extended periods.

I've watched him deliver amazing sales growth results for many of our clients, coaching hundreds of sales leaders and sales reps to grit their teeth, engage outside of their comfort zones, and do it long enough to enjoy the success that flows from focus and consistency.

His ability to coach success across large groups is tightly linked to the simplicity of the programs he helps clients develop.

As Einstein noted, "Everything should be made as simple as possible, but no simpler."

This book makes new business development simple, and that is its genius. That simplicity makes it easy for those willing to do the work, follow the time-efficient plan, and make it a daily habit.

This book is not the next shiny promise. It is a manual for sales growth including everything you need to plan and execute.

I wish you the very best in your sales career, and I hope you can keep things simple enough, to truly enjoy all the success a career in sales has to offer.

Dean Mannix
Co-Founder & CEO SalesITV

Introduction

If you've picked up this book, you're probably interested in how to be more effective at selling. You might want to get better at selling yourself, or you might be looking for strategies that will help your team become better sellers.

Whether you're selling yourself or leading a team of reps, you can use the outbound strategies in this book to boost your or your team's response rates. In a matter of weeks, you'll find that you're having more sales conversations with your ideal clients. You'll also be spending far less time chasing those go-nowhere soft maybes. How you use the time you'll be saving is up to you. Perhaps you'll spend it with your family; perhaps you'll pour that extra time and energy into building your personal brand. However you use your time, you'll soon have more of it.

I'm going to let you in on a secret about sales books. Most of them are not written with reps in mind. Most sales books are a means to an end. They are written to secure more consulting work for the author. They are written with sales managers in mind—not those who are actually doing the selling. Most sales books are little more than platforms for consultants to show how neatly they align with current sales wisdom. If they dovetail neatly with the mindset of senior sales leaders, the author will be rolling in consulting fees for years.

Those who actually read and use the books are an after-thought. If you're looking to become a more successful seller, only a small handful of books out there will help you do this. This is one of those books.

I have written this book with frontline sellers in the front of my mind. The majority of my work is with these infantrymen of sales, so this is what I'm most interested in and qualified to talk about. What you hold in your hands is a working guide, a handbook for those who need to complete transactions and complete them frequently. It is an instruction manual for reps who need to make calls, pay visits, and send emails and other electronic communications both to prospects and to their existing clients. It is a toolkit for reps who need to find and engage with new prospects and want to do so in ways that are ethical, repeatable and personally scalable—all without putting their carefully curated personal brand at risk.

What you'll find here is straightforward advice. I'm going to tell you what to do and how to do it. Other authors in this space might tell you to *lead with insights* or to *lead with value*, but they don't get down to brass tacks and actually talk about what leading with insights or with value actually looks like.

To do this, I've provided significant resources at the back of the book, including phone scripts, email templates, and much more. You'll also find information on how to reach out to prospects on LinkedIn—a form of outreach that has been a powerful driver of my success and the success of my clients.

I don't just want you to read this book. I want you to use it. Write in it, highlight sections and stick Post-it Notes in it. I want you to take meaningful action (the only thing that can truly impact your results). The advice in these pages has been responsible for my success. These strategies have helped me grow my consulting business and, no matter what you're selling, they can help you as well.

Methodology

Ask reps and sales leaders about their sales situation. Chances are, they will tell you that theirs is entirely unique. It might be their product, their market niche, their customers, or some mixture of the three, but *something* is making their job particularly difficult or even (so they say) impossible. I'm going to break a few hearts: your products, prospects, or markets aren't all that unique. No matter what their industry, reps come to me with the same questions, and I don't radically adjust my responses to fit their niche or their product. At their root, the problems are the same, and so are their solutions.

No matter what you're selling or to whom, your sales situations are predictable. This means that, when we know what to do and say and how to do it and say it, success is also predictable and repeatable.

We can plan, rehearse, and tweak our approach so we are prepared for the barriers and objections we'll inevitably encounter. The more we prepare, the more we can be present in the conversation and impact its tempo. Making it up as you go along won't work—especially not with the challenges today's reps are facing. You need a plan.

I didn't discover the relationship between preparation and success on my own—it had to be drilled into me. I spent three and a half years in the Australian Army as an assault trooper with the Second Cavalry Regiment. On my first day, it became immediately clear that I had a relevant skill baseline of zero. I had to learn how to move before I could learn to win. Starting from zero, incrementally, I improved my skills.

One of the first skills I learned was the importance of preparation and rehearsal. We were taught to field strip (disassemble) and reassemble our SLRs (L1A1 Self-Loading Rifles) inside 30 seconds. We did this over and over again until we could literally do it blindfolded. The concept was, if we needed to conduct emergency repairs on our combat rifles in the dark, we could.

The Army taught me that it doesn't matter who you are or what your background is. It doesn't matter whether you're tall or short, slim or not so slim, very young or not so very young. The Army's training is a machine that produces prepared and capable soldiers. It does this through the deliberate pre-planning and rehearsal of combat situations. When the situations are no longer simulated, the trained soldier reverts to his or her training. They make the right decisions when they are under fire because they *know* what to do. They've done it before, countless times. It's muscle memory in action.

> **It's easy to do your job well when everything is going well. Only those who are prepared can continue to perform even when conditions deteriorate. This is the definition of high performance.**

The training routines and the level of preparedness they instilled in me have remained with me. They have been the foundation of my success as a civilian on the corporate battlefield. I leverage these strategies when I train reps and sales managers. Through preparation, I help reps clear away the fog of war, allowing them to emerge from their everyday sales battles victorious.

The processes I introduce to reps in my training sessions are the same processes you'll find in these pages. I've built a considerable reputation on the backs of these processes and the results they reliably produce for my clients. They've helped me grow my consulting and training company from nothing in 2014 to a highly profitable business, and they are the sole reason that, in 2016, LinkedIn ranked me as the number one Australian Social Seller on LinkedIn. Just as they've worked for me, they'll work for you.

Introducing the Cadence

At the centre of the strategies that we'll be looking at in this book is the cadence. The cadence is a planned and deliberate series of multi-channel outreaches. Implemented properly, the cadence substantially increases prospect reply rates and lead qualifications. A cadence might last for nine weeks, but it doesn't take that long to start working. It starts producing results (i.e., collaborative communication with our prospects) almost immediately.

For the purpose of this book, the cadence I use here assumes an outbound strategy. Whilst a cadence-based approach will certainly help when trying to engage with inbound leads, I don't cover them specifically in this book.

> **When building a cadence For inbound leads, use these same strategies; however, use a much higher attempt frequency and a shorter duration (up to 10 attempts in 7 days across multiple channels).**

Finally, the cadence is also a strategy purpose built for B2B sales (the vast majority of my work is in B2B, so it's where my experience and expertise lie). The strategies we'll cover in this book have proven effectiveness when it comes to starting conversations with B2B prospects, generating follow-up calls, booking product demos, and organising meetings. B2C reps have used the cadence and benefitted from its deliberate, multi-channel outreach (starting more conversations and booking more appointments), but, if you're a B2C rep, you'll notice that the language I use in this book is clearly aimed at B2B reps.

We'll look at what a cadence is and how we build one in much more detail a little later on, but for now let's answer the burning question:

Who will benefit from using a cadence?

A cadence will help anyone who needs to reach out to prospective clients in order to grow their organisation's revenue. This might include account managers, business development professionals, CEOs who sell, entrepreneurs, customer success professionals, SDRs, inside sales reps, business owners and more—really, anybody whose success depends on their ability to start conversations with potential clients and bring these conversations to a successful conclusion. For simplicity's sake, I'll refer to this grab bag of sales professionals as 'reps'. This includes anybody who is out there, on the front lines, representing their organisations.

All of the examples we'll cover in this book assume that you have other responsibilities to balance with your sales activities. Most reps are simultaneously responsible for developing new business and serving existing clients. The result is often a struggle to find the time and resources to sell effectively.

Many of the reps I encounter tell me that they *get around* to reaching out to new clients when they're not busy serving existing ones. This approach has always concerned me, simply because the results it produces are predictably poor.

7

New business doesn't get its fair share of the rep's time and mindshare, so it slows to a trickle.

I understand the time crunch that today's reps are facing, but I also know that no business can survive that doesn't place some emphasis on outreach. There is a balance to be struck between the two, and I know it's not as easily done as said.

Your cadence is built with this time crunch in mind. I've made it a simple and straightforward process, so you can start building a cadence from scratch with very little preparation. All the tools and templates for mapping out your time and outreach processes are included in the back of the book. You'll also find additional resources on my website: **www.markmc.co/tpg**

Chapter 1

The New Rules of Engagement

T oday's reps are working in an environment that is tough-
er than it has ever been. It's our job (as it always has
been) to start conversations with prospects, introducing
them and their organisations to our products and services.
We pick up the phone and call our prospects or drive over to
their office. However, over the last two decades, the rules of
engagement have changed.

Privacy laws and anti-spam legislation (including the
Australian Spam Act of 2003) have made these rules
concrete. The General Data Protection Regulation (GDPR)
came into effect across the EU and EEA on May 25th, 2018.
It is the most robust SPAM benchmark on the planet, and
it has changed the way outreach is conducted in Europe.
The California Consumer Privacy Act (CCPA) was updated
in 2020 to further tighten the net, making it less and less
acceptable to send unsolicited outreach electronically.

The result of all this legislation: less space for unethical and spammy operators (undeniably a good thing). Reps who are successful in this climate are not broadcasting low-quality messages far and wide. Instead, they are focusing all of their efforts on high-quality outreach.

And legislation is only one of the barriers reps have to navigate. Filtering and blocking software is giving buyers more and more power over their inboxes. The result is tumbling email campaign effectiveness. According to 2019 Mailchimp data, email open rates are 21.33 percent. Four out of five outreach emails get pushed into spam or trash folders, where they either remain unopened or are immediately deleted.

There are still gaps we can shimmy through, but we simply won't get through them with poorly targeted and poorly planned outreach. The quality of the message *is* the message.

> **The quality of the message *is* the message.**

Not too long ago, the going wisdom was that sales is just a numbers game. Success meant hitting your numbers. There was an acceptable levels of prospect dissatisfaction in this approach. This is, we said, the price that reps pay to play in the big game. This no longer works. The days of throwing it all at the wall and seeing what sticks are far behind us. It's no longer a feasible outreach strategy. Successful digital and social selling reps don't send poor outreach into the ether. They know that their brands (personal and organisational) are always tentative. Few things can damage a brand faster than a spammy campaign (or, even worse, a string of them). The move away from quantity outreach to that of quality is how we make sure that our outreach strengthens rather than weakens our brands.

According to 2014 IDC Research data, three quarters of B2B buyers now use social research during their buying journey. A spammy campaign with your name attached to it will get eyes on your LinkedIn profile—and not the kind you want. It's no longer possible to hide behind a corporate email account. For better or worse, we can see our prospects, but they can also see us.

The result of all of this is confusion. Reps are uncertain about what they can and can't and should and shouldn't do. They want to align their outreach with what prospects expect, but they aren't certain what these expectations are. With the stakes as high as they are, reps have dug into their foxholes, where they sit, frozen in indecision.

Top-Down Confusion

These problems aren't limited to reps. Many sales leaders are just as confused as those they lead. Sales leaders know the game has changed; when they compare the ways they themselves buy with the ways their organisation is selling, they can see clear misalignment. Even if they don't have this level of awareness, their poor sales numbers will tell them that something is wrong.

Those old strategies of cold calling and cold emailing simply don't work anymore. According to a 2019 CSO Insights sales performance study, only 52 percent of reps regularly hit their quotas, and the sales team's effectiveness remains challenged across several fronts. Sales leaders know they need to encourage their reps to try something new, but they are unsure what to do.

Sales leaders know that the key that fits all locks is the high-quality sales conversation, but they also know that this key has changed shape over the last few years. What made them successful when they were reps now falls flat. Their experience, learned in the trenches, is no longer applicable.

At a loss for new approaches to these problems, many sales leaders are falling back into what used to work. They are amplifying the signal. They're prescribing a blanket approach to more poor activity—missing the appropriate solution by miles. Results refuse to budge. Staff are demotivated, clients and prospects alienated, and personal and professional brands are damaged.

A significant number of sales organisations that I work with tell me that finding new prospects who are willing to communicate with them remains the most difficult part of their sales process. Finding someone to engage with has never been easy, but the changing rules of engagement have made it more difficult. No matter how good we are at negotiating and handling objections, these skills don't mean jack squat unless we can first find prospects who are willing to talk to us.

It doesn't matter what industry or sector you work in, the concerns are the same. I've seen these challenges first hand in sectors such as Fin-Tech, Fin-Services, Technology, Telco, FMCG (Fast Moving Consumer Goods), Business Services,

Hospitality, SaaS, and more. All cite the same concerns. They're having difficulty starting conversations.

Day in and day out, I hear the same questions from reps:

➜   Is my outreach annoying my clients? Am I coming off as spammy or spooky? How is this affecting my personal brand?

➜   Is my sales activity enough?

➜   Am I giving up too early? How do I know when to give up on a prospect?

➜   What message should I use to reach out to my prospects?

➜   When is the best time to call? When is the best time to email?

➜   How should I be integrating social into my outreach?

➜   How long should I wait between outreach attempts?

➜   What messaging channel should I use?

Reps are generally focused on how they are perceived in the marketplace and by their employers. They are struggling to balance the expectations of one with the other (trying to meet their quotas without damaging their personal brands). They tend to err on the side of personal brand conservation (one of the reasons that quota numbers are in the gutter). Rather than risk damaging their brands, they're letting their activity levels drop. This means that reps aren't spending enough time having conversations.

Sales leaders have related but different concerns. They too recognise that sales outreach has changed, and they're slowly coming around to the idea that the old *do more* approach simply isn't working. They're also aware that there needs to be a high level of rep buy-in that covers the entire prospecting process. The new generation of reps don't respond well to commands from on high. They want to feel (and see) that what they're doing is meaningful. Without widespread buy-in, sales departments simply spin their wheels in the mud.

Sales leaders come to me with the following points of concern:

➔   How do I get my team to embrace prospecting?

➔   How do I get reps to conduct enough sales activity?

➔   How do I get reps on the same page? How can I make sure reps are all using the same messages?

➔   How will a new outreach strategy affect our brand?

➔   How can I make my reps more successful? How can I convince them that their success is important to the organisation?

➔   How can we create systems and process with widespread buy-in from both reps and managers?

I've found that a carefully defined and agreed-upon contact strategy helps reps and their managers answer these questions definitively and in ways that satisfy them both. Armed with the right strategy, they can navigate through the twenty-first century direct sales landscape and its shifting rules of engagement.

We call this strategy the cadence.

We've Got a Communication Problem

Communication has changed. Few sales organisations have adapted to new communication preferences. This has dramatically reduced outreach effectiveness. We need something that gains the attention of our prospects and helps us start a meaningful conversation. We need a fluid approach to sales communication, and without a cadence, we don't have one.

If you've been in sales for more than a few years, you've learned that the sales game is highly dynamic. Nothing stays the same for very long. There is always a new methodology, some new technology, or some new way to sell that seems to be gaining traction. This is largely driven by our prospects' constantly shifting preferences. A spammy campaign might have once slid off our prospects' backs, but now, on the spectrum of acceptable behaviours, sending spammy, unsolicited messages sits somewhere between farting in elevators and driving drunk—very undesirable.

Few things illustrate the degree of these changes quite

like the telephone. You probably remember the sound of the phone ringing in your home. Landlines once delivered important messages—so important that the sound of a ringing phone required an immediate response. Today, only a third of Australians (most of them seniors) have a landline in their home. The sound of a ringing phone (if it's heard at all) doesn't carry the same degree of immediacy that it once did. It's background noise. Calls go unanswered. Muted phones and call blocking are commonplace. For many people, if you're not in their address book, you're not getting through, period.

Similar changes have happened to email, social outreach, and just about every other communication medium you can think of. Email is less effective than ever. Many businesses are moving away from email for their internal communication and into more secure services like Slack, Trello or Microsoft Teams. Spam filters (especially in large organisations) are blocking our messages. Around 80 percent of emails never see the light of day, and email response rates are desperately low (single-digit percentages and moving towards decimal points).

For most of us, the largest issue is one surrounding volume. Those who are responsible for the type of buying decisions we're looking for are facing an onslaught of messages. Steuart Snooks, known to many as Australia's email guru, tells me that the executives he helps often receive in excess of 150 emails per day. If we're going to use email as a form of outreach, we need to find ways to stand out in these crowded inboxes.

Social outreach (once the secret sauce of effective twenty-first-century prospecting) is now home to the same kind of spammy sellers that have made the phone and emails so much more difficult to use. LinkedIn is still one of the best ways to start valuable conversations outside of the conventional channels, but we now have to compete with the worst elements of the business community. A pitch-perfect conversation via InMail or a well-worded connection request can still be like adding rocket fuel to your backyard bonfire, but we need to lift our voices above the spammers, endless junk connection requests, and sponsored InMails with (at best) questionable relevance. We need to develop credibility quickly, and we're fighting against intensifying currents of caution and scepticism.

What's more, we can no longer be successful in a single channel. Reps who call, call and call, or those who send strings of emails are not seen as trustworthy or innovative. They are seen as just another commodity supplier or, worse, just another spammer. If they do manage to get through and win their prospects' attention, they'll have to ward off pricing challenges. They're at the bottom of the sales totem pole.

Communication Breakthrough: The Cadence

A defined and deliberate cadence supported with great messaging steps around these communication problems by creating a point of difference—a touchstone of intrigue. Reps approach prospects not as servants but as peers. This places them in a much stronger position when they start negotiating conversation time and having pricing conversations.

The cadence is scheduled across a multi-week timeframe, with predetermined frequency and multi-channel touch points built into its structure. The multi-channel approach is particularly important. More than anything else, it is this that sets reps apart from the crowd of spammers and cold callers.

Not only will the cadence guide when you communicate and through which channel, it will also guide each conversation (you'll find all the scripts you'll need at the end of this book). All of this combines to make the process highly effective and entirely repeatable.

Reps using the cadence can know, and know for certain, that they are doing enough of the right activity at the right times. They'll know that they're doing what they need to do to start and continue those valuable conversation, and they'll be generating sales, usually in the range of four to eight touches. They'll know they're in the goldilocks zone between too much and too little activity. They'll know their personal brands are safe.

Not only will reps have new confidence, the sales leaders who manage them will enjoy new levels of confidence in their reps and their sales activities. The cadence alleviates their fears around low team activity and protects the professional brands their reps and their organisations have worked so hard to develop. It does this whilst providing a clear and achievable set of outbound expectations for the team to work towards.

It's clear, effective, and repeatable. It's the key that fits every lock.

Chapter 2
Change or Die

The sales environment is changing, and the challenges are not always client or prospect driven. Increased complexity inside our own sales organisations has made time dedicated to sales activities more precious than ever. The changing nature of our organisations has increased the number of roles (think sales development reps and sales enablement teams). With more people from our side involved in the buyer's journey, sales have increased in complexity. Sales enablement and sales ops functions have added more and more tech to navigate. Some of this is truly helpful, but the time it takes to navigate this new environment impacts the available selling time.

We are spending less time selling and more time organising and reporting. Most reps spend around one third of their time on core sales activities, including meetings with new prospects and prospecting. Sales leaders, who also live in this new landscape, have less and less time for their important coaching duties. We can't create time out of thin air, so if we want to sell more, we need a way to do more with less. We need to make the absolute most of the time that we do have available for core selling activities.

We need to remember as well that complexity has also increased on the client side of the equation. Harvard Business Review researchers said in 2017 that, at that time, there was an average of 6.8 decision makers in a typical B2B sales exchange, and this number has probably risen since then. With each decision maker added to the process, it becomes harder and harder to gain consensus. Vendors are standing shoulder-to-shoulder in a crowded marketplace, making it difficult for buyers to tell the good from the bad.

The result is buyers who have essentially taken matters into their own hands. They are doing significantly more research, relying less and less on reps to guide them towards an informed buying decision. According to recent CSO Insights data, nearly 80 percent of buyers report that they don't see reps as a problem-solving resource, and 70 percent of buyers only engage with reps when they are closing in on the end of their buying journey. By this time, their minds are almost entirely made up.

We are being pushed to the sidelines. All of our training is premised on the belief that reps can be (and *should be*) a valuable part of the buying process, but we now need to do more to convince buyers that we are trustworthy partners.

And this isn't all! There are a number of other big changes that require equally large solutions. Let's take a closer look at each of them.

Change #1: Evaporating Sales Effectiveness

Companies expect revenue to increase steadily, but conventional forms of outreach are becoming less and less effective with each passing day. More of the same simply won't cut it. According to a 2019 Salesforce report on the state of sales, 57 percent of sellers expect to miss their quotas.

> **57 percent of reps expect to miss their quotas.**
> **Reps report that their #1 challenge is a lack of leads.**

Sales effectiveness and the confidence that comes with it are in freefall. Underperforming sales reps are quick to blame the quality of the leads (some things never change), but the heart of the issue lies elsewhere. More leads won't solve the problem—it's only doubling down on a bad bet.

Change #2: Movement Towards Customer-centric Messaging

Pestering your prospects into submission doesn't work anymore. Clients expect (or are pleasantly surprised by) interactions that add value. If we can do this, we'll be at the front of their minds throughout their buying journey. The first rep who interacts with a buyer in a meaningful way is more likely to be chosen as the winning partner. A barrage of check-in phone calls or a slew of lazy emails might get noticed, but it will be for all the wrong reasons.

Bringing commercial perspective to your prospect conversations is the new value-currency that reps need to bring to their early client interactions. If you continue to push for low-value engagements just for the sake of making contact, you'll slide down the food chain. You'll end up as a bottom feeder. The only conversations you'll be having will be with buyers who either cannot or will not make a decision.

Remember, regardless of where you enter the sales conversation in an organisation, you will quickly be delegated down to the level that you *sound* like. If you sound like a commodity, you'll be delegated down to the level of a commodity supplier. If we start high-level, commercially important conversations, we stay higher in the organisation. This is where the strategic conversations take place, and it's where we want to be.

The costs of a spammy or rude outreach are higher than ever. Hard-earned goodwill can go up in flames in an instant. Irrelevant boilerplate can quickly result in that LinkedIn post that every rep secretly fears: the shaming complaint post. Your prospect takes your poorly conceived outreach and posts it on LinkedIn, flaming you for everybody to see. The post gets shared and commented on. In an instant, you're infamous.

It's no wonder that reps today have a steely-eyed focus on the protection of their personal brand—as, indeed, they should. They're frozen in fear and indecision. Better to do nothing than to risk burning the whole thing down.

If your message isn't customer-centric, it's not going to get noticed or, worse, it will get noticed, but for the wrong reasons.

Rather than addressing your market with scattershot, build a narrative that hits your prospect square between the eyes. Talk to them and address their pain points in an undeniably accurate way. Make your messages truly customer-centric and then they'll be banging down your door (and they'll leave the torches and pitchforks at home).

Change #3: Oversaturation

When sales outreach came to us via just one or two channels, we could handle it. In the last two decades, though, sales outreach has started to come at us from every direction. Our prospects are digging further and further down into their bunkers. The barrage never stops, though, and our shell-shocked prospects are tuning our messaging out.

We've crossed the saturation point, and there's no going back.

How many uncleared messages do you have in your inbox? Most people have hundreds. Some have thousands across multiple email accounts. And that's just a single channel. We've also got text messages and social media, our internal chat platforms, messaging programs, and CRM chats. All of these messages require some action (even if it's only deletion).

How do we deal with this degree of saturation? We compartmentalise, responding only to those message that demand our immediate attention. We need to find a way to get out to the front of our prospects' minds—to get past the compartmentalisation barriers.

Change #4: Tech Barriers

Technology has made it easier to find and reach out to prospects, but it's also given our prospects new tools that make it easier for them to avoid our calls (think about how caller ID made our jobs more difficult overnight).

Thanks to block and mute functions, it's easier than ever for prospects to ignore us entirely. Buyers are in almost complete control of communication frequency, which means they can speed up or slow down the conversation as and when they like. In short, like never before, they control the transaction.

Professional buyers, who face a never-ending barrage of outreach, have become experts at the non-reply. New technologies like pixel/image disablement and the movement away from email and towards internal messaging systems will make it even easier for buyers to keep outreach off to one side, and even harder for us to get through their barriers.

We need to find a way through these barriers whilst there are still gaps wide enough to shimmy through.

Rapid Change = Rep Discouragement

All of this change has produced a climate in which sales can feel like a losing game. It's hard to overstate just how much the resulting discouragement influences the results we can expect. By and large, sales managers give sales reps the tools they need to sell effectively, but they overlook motivation and let discouragement slip under their radar.

Reps are becoming increasingly less effective. As it becomes more difficult to start and continue meaningful conversations with prospects, reps find it more and more difficult to pick up the phone or to compose an attention-grabbing message. Their productivity drops, and this only adds to their discouragement.

Struggling reps blame the leads or, even worse, the product. Rather than adapting to the new sales climate, they go in search of greener pastures. They look for a new employer or, in some cases, an entirely different profession. Nobody wants to feel like a failure, and the new generation of professionals entering the workforce doesn't have the patience to deal with constant rejection. They want success, and they want it as fast as possible. They want to feel that they're making an impact, and instead they feel like they're banging on a closed door.

This discouragement and its consequences are bad news all around. Talented reps have tremendous earning potential, both for themselves and for their employers. Each time one of these gifted sellers leaves their employer or, even worse, the industry, they are closing a door on that potential. There are no winners in this scenario—only losers.

At the same time, many reps have spent years banging at that door and, so far, it's refused to open for them. It's only natural for them to move to the next door down the line. If we want to battle this discouragement, we need to give them the key that opens the door to higher levels of achievement. This means giving them a process that includes clearly defined steps that can help them make their outreach more successful.

When that door finally swings open on its hinges and reps start realising their selling potential, months or even years of pent-up discouragement can evaporate in an instant.

Changing the Message

One of the first things we need to do if we want to start encouraging rather than discouraging reps is change the message. We need to change the message in two ways—the first focused on reps, the second focused on prospects.

The Message for Reps: Consistently Good Beats Occasionally Great

Reps need to hear—and hear it loud and clear—that consistently good beats occasionally great every day of the week and twice on Sunday. This message applies equally to teams and to individuals.

> **"Consistently good always beats occasionally great."**
> —*Dean Mannix*

Over the years, I've worked with reps from one end of the talent spectrum to the other. What separates the highest performers from the lowest is consistency. Like clockwork, the top performers do the same things (the right things) at crucial moments in their outreach. Rarely is sales success the result of a single piece of sales-brilliance. Rather, it is the cumulative effect of being consistently good across all aspects of the sales process.

Conversely, sales failures are rarely the result of one cataclysmic mistake. Deals fall through and reps drop out because unchecked inconsistencies have crept into our systems and processes. There are countless symptoms of inconsistency: coming late to the office, failure to lock in prospecting time (the *I'll get to it when I have a spare minute* approach), a lack of pitch rehearsal, unpredictable pricing variation, or wild variations in presentation quality. When we are inconsistent, even if we are occasionally great, we will be judged more for these consistent failures than for our occasional wins.

The Message for Prospects: "We understand you"

The goal of outreach is to secure further interest and, eventually, meetings (face to face or virtual) with our ideal clients. When we are consistently good at prospecting, we will have a pipeline positively brimming with qualified prospects and opportunities. We get there by placing the customer at the very centre of our outreach.

Most of the reps I speak to want to do this and, more than this, they want to do it honestly and ethically. They don't want to rely on false pretences or exaggerations. Instead, they want to have meaningful and honest conversations with prospects. They just don't quite know how to start these conversations.

We start these conversations by showing the customer that we understand them. We need to show them that we understand their issues, but also that we understand how they want to be communicated with. We'll look more at this second point later on, but let's take a closer look at the first point.

Customer-centric messaging means a connection premised on an offer of value to the client. If you're focused on *your* solution, you're not addressing your prospects in customer-centric ways. What prompts them to give you their attention and, eventually, their business has to be *their* reason, not ours.

> **"When you sell hammers, everything looks like a nail."**
> —*Salesism*

This is a crucial distinction, and it's at the heart of so many of our outreach failures. When we ask our prospects for 15 minutes of their time for them to tell us about their business, we are doing them a double disservice. First, we're lying to them. Effective discovery calls rarely take less than 30 or 45 minutes. Second, think about what we are asking our client to do here. We are asking them to stop their day (even it is only for 15 minutes) and tell us about their business so we can find a reason they need what we're selling.

This isn't customer-centric. You need to *start* the conversation by showing them that you understand them (not come to understand them over the course of the call). Let me give you an example:

> *"Because we work with a lot of HR leaders in tech, we know that there is a focus on the growing IT skills gap and what that means to both the sales function (securing the available revenue) and in the capacity space (can you complete what you need to in time?).*
>
> *We know that there are five common mistakes most firms are making in relation to talent attraction. These mistakes are stopping good candidates from applying for your roles.*
>
> *Would it be a good idea to grab a chat about those five things?"*

If tech companies make up a sizable portion of my market, I should know that the IT skills gap has been a thorn in their side for some time. As a result of this skills gap, they struggle to fill those empty roles and this impacts their ability to complete projects, increases pressure on wages, and makes it harder for them to grow in line with the size of the overall market.

With a foothold in these kinds of specific issues, we can shape our messaging to hit them square between the eyes. We're offering them a chance to engage on something that is important to them. We have valuable information they want. They feel seen. They feel as though we know them.

When we combine this kind of messaging with a disciplined and consistent multi-channel approach, we can set ourselves apart from the crowd. We can sell honestly and ethically, and we can be spectacularly successful in our roles. Sales may have changed, but so long as we change with it and adapt to our prospects' shifting expectations, we can adapt to the new climate and excel in it.

Chapter 3
The Five Pillars of Effective Prospecting

Before we turn to building a cadence, we need to build out the foundations. We need to understand what makes an outreach campaign successful in the kind of climate I outlined in the last chapter. There are five pillars of effective prospecting:

1. Mindset

2. Smart Targeting

3. Smart Messaging

4. Multi-Channel

5. Sequence

5 Pillars of Prospecting

- Personal beliefs
- Rep's compelling story
- Accountability

MINDSET

- IDEAL clients
- ICP built tight
- Personas dialed
- Priorities & challenges understood

SMART TARGETING

5 PILLARS OF PROSPECTING

- Across what duration
- Frequency of outreach
- Total volume

SEQUENCE

SMART MESSAGING

- Quality not quantity
- Preferred communication channels
- Personalised
- Leverages influence

MULTI-CHANNEL

- Multi-channel touches
- Multi-touch per attempt
- 3 or more channels used

How we approach these pillars will impact our ability to build out a successful cadence and therefore a successful outreach campaign. In this chapter (the longest in this book), we'll look at each of the five pillars in detail, starting with mindset.

Pillar 1: Mindset

I'm always surprised at the number of reps who tell me they love going out and speaking to prospective clients. They're excited to discuss commercial outcomes with prospects and to grow their network of industry connections. Yet, at the same time, they are reluctant to start these conversations and build these connections. They see their own outreach as a nuisance, and they don't want to interrupt or disturb their prospects. There is a massive disconnect.

Common Mindset Mistakes

1   Prioritising: Although it should be their top priority, reps consistently put other activities before business development.

2   Miscalculating: Reps convince themselves they are doing more business development work than they are actually doing.

Anybody who has ever been on the front line of sales knows that outreach can feel uncomfortable, but discomfort is the price reps have to pay to access those meaningful conversations. We can't cross that bridge without paying the toll. I promise, the conversations will get easier (and more comfortable) as we get deeper and deeper into the cadence, but we need to brace ourselves for some initial discomfort.

To do this, we first need to align our mindset with our goals. This means truly believing in what you're selling. You need to look beyond your product's features or benefits. You need to be conscious of how your product makes a real difference to your prospects' commercial outcomes. When you truly believe in the commercial value of what you're selling, you will be more willing to push through any preliminary discomfort to uncover the quality conversation beyond it.

> **In order to sell anything,**
> **we must first sell ourselves.**

If you're scared of rejection or afraid of failure, you're not alone. We all start out tentatively, but those of us who have survived in this industry have learned to take action, even when we're scared. What's the worst that can happen? Maybe a prospect ghosts you, maybe they hang up on you. This is simply part of the job. Own it and mentally prepare for it as an integral part of the sales process.

If we are only prepared to do what others do, we will only ever be as successful as they are (and maybe not even that much). In order to get the results we want, we need to be willing to do what others will not. This means interrupting the pattern—causing a glitch in our prospects' matrix.

We are trying to change their thinking patterns—this has long been the goal of sales—but we're also trying to break their more recently developed patterns of reflexively deleting outreach. If we want the opportunity to change how they think, we need to first change how we think.

> **The 30-Day Rule**
> "The prospecting you do in this 30-day period
> will pay off for the next 90 days."
> —*Jeb Blount*

The response we get won't always be positive, but a quick and clear *no* is far better than a long drawn-out one. We need to be willing, from the outset, to strive for that clear answer, even if it's a negative one. Of course, that *yes* is music to our ears, but our next-favourite sound should be that clear, decisive *no*.

Nothing gums up the works of our outreach quite like the slow *no* or the drawn out *maybe*. We often allow prospects to string us along because we are afraid of the rejection that, deep down, we know is coming. We end up with a pipeline full of maybes. We waste our time and theirs by following up infrequently and softly, scared to uncover a *no*. If they haven't said *no*, that means we've still got a chance right? Wrong.

The vast majority of outreach follows this pattern, and we need to be comfortable with the fact that not everyone we talk to will be a perfect fit for us. We can let them go their way, and we can go ours.

All reps suffer from what I call *sellers' bias*. It's sellers' bias that keeps us from pushing beyond that soft *maybe*. We are biased against ourselves. We convince ourselves that every non-response is a personal rebuff. We lump ourselves in with all the other spammy and pushy reps out there and hesitate when we should be taking action. We forget about the value we bring to our prospects. We belittle ourselves and negate the power of our outreach. This negative bias is a cancer that, if you let it, will eat away at your confidence and your motivation.

> **Beware of Sellers' Bias**
> Don't see yourself or your outreach as a nuisance.
> Challenge your limiting beliefs.

It's sellers' bias that keeps us from calling prospects at times we might think are inconvenient for them (e.g., before nine in the morning or over the lunch hour). It's the same self-doubt that is keeping us from spreading our outreach into multiple channels. This is the mindset that keeps us from having quality sales conversations. Even if we're spending our time on outreach, it's not time well spent.

With the right mindset, you'll never be reluctant to deliberately pursue your dream customers. You'll see yourself (and they'll see you) as a value-providing partner. You'll know that every conversation you start has the potential to deliver valuable business outcomes. Knowing this, and knowing it deep down, changes everything.

When you start articulating value in this way, you'll move from making outreach to telling a compelling story—and we never feel discomfort when we're telling a great story, and neither do our prospects (especially when they're the hero of the story).

No matter who we're talking to, when we have a compelling story to tell, we feel like we belong in the conversation. We move from talking about products and features to talking about valuable outcomes.

Think back to when you first joined your organisation. Think about when you told your mum or your spouse about the company. You probably framed the organisation as the best possible place for you to be. You were excited to sell for the organisation because you believed in its products and their value. Replicate those types of conversations with your prospects and you'll be telling that personal, compelling story that rises above the sales static. Each time you tell the story, you'll get better at telling it.

What's my compelling story? I believe sales is a truly great occupation when you have the right skills, tools and the mindset to succeed. It is also one of the most challenging roles when you're not performing. I know that life sucks when you're an underperforming rep. Stress, pressure, self doubt, long hours, low income and poor confidence make the daily grind almost unbearable for struggling reps.

> **Get the NO.**
> Other than a quick *yes*,
> a quick *no* is the best answer you can get.
> A slow *maybe* is your worst enemy.

Conversely, life as a rep on or above quota is great. They display high levels of confidence and strong job satisfaction levels, management tends to let them get on with the job, and they enjoy financial rewards commensurate with their input.

The difference is huge, but the performance gap between an average rep and a successful one is quite small. I love helping reps make that leap so that they and the organisation they work for both get what they want out of the relationship. The more people I can help close that gap, the better this industry will be for all of us.

I feel confident talking to senior sellers and business owners because I know my work brings value—and lots of it. They all want happier, more productive sales reps and the increased revenue that comes with that, and their reps want the same thing. I've made this benefit the heart of my compelling story, and because I believe in it, I have no problem sharing my story with prospects of all kinds.

All of this would be impossible without the right mindset. Remember that all sales are made above the neck. This sales game truly is a headcase.

Pillar 2: Smart Targeting

Remember that, no matter how good your messages are, they will only be partially effective if you are not hitting the right prospects right between the eyes. The deeper your understanding of your prospects and their particular problems, the more effective your cadence and your outreach will be. We need more than simple targeting. We need smart targeting.

Let's say that you sell business software and that dentists are one of your primary customer targets. If we focus on dentists as a group, that's still a helicopter view. It's a start, but we need to get much closer than this if we want to be effective. Let's start by narrowing it down geographically. Let's say your ideal customers are dentists who, not only have their own practice, but are located within 25km of your office. You will quickly find a bunch of very similar attributes amongst all the dentists who meet these criteria. They will use the same language, have the same concerns and challenges, be accessible at the same time of the day, and respond to the same types of messages. They probably struggle with last-minute cancellations and no-shows. They might have to complete staff development and admin outside of surgery hours. They might be interested in finding other dentists to work for them to increase their billing capacity, or they might be interested in significantly growing their customer base.

> *"Hi Bob,*
> *I've been working with several dentists in Eastern Sydney, and I keep hearing the same three challenges from them.*
>
> *1) No-shows*
>
> *2) Last-minute cancellations*
>
> *3) Client volume variations*
>
> *Does this sound like you? Or are you on top of the situation and achieving a 90 percent+ efficiency rate in your practice's billable hours?"*

With even a broad understanding of their specific problems (a little research goes a long way), you can start to probe deeper and uncover some of their more specific issues.

Some of these problems might be entirely unique, but a good number of them will be common to the businesses that you've chosen to target in your area. The sooner you can place your finger on these issues, the more your reputation as an expert will grow.

Your outreach grows more powerful when you start with your prospects already in focus—the zooming in will help you capture the smaller details that others miss.

> **To make your targeting smarter, work a specific client sector for 90 days. The smarter your targeting, the easier it becomes to build prospect lists, find credible reasons to engage, and start meaningful conversations.**

Why are prospecting messages dismissed as spam? Because they are transparently focused on the seller's goals, not on the recipients. Front and centre in the message is the request—a phone call, a product demonstration, a meeting, or an outright request to purchase. These messages are no sooner seen than they are deleted (and, often, the seller is blocked). If we want to convince the prospect that our messages are not spam, we need to stop thinking about what we, as reps, want to achieve. Instead, we need to use our messaging to show the prospect that we see them, their challenges, and their goals, and we need to show them that this is what we are focused on. In this approach, we're not asking them to buy but for a chance to explore further.

I've found that prospects in similar positions share more than just problems. They also share communication preferences. When we can bring our prospects into focus, we can make some educated guesses about which channels they prefer and how they like to be approached in these channels. This will allow us to reach out with considerably more -certainty.

Let me give you a few examples. Sales leaders (directors, managers, etc.) are much more likely to pick up a ringing phone than those in marketing or HR. Why? Because they've been using the phone to communicate with customers for years, and old habits die hard. They reach for that handset almost reflexively. After all, the call could be from an existing client or even a new client.

Understanding this specific nuance makes it possible to make a more educated calculation about what will work with a given prospect. It makes sense to weight our cadence towards phone calls if we're trying to reach sales leaders. If we're trying to reach somebody in marketing or HR, we can expect emails or social outreach to be more successful. Mapping preferences like this makes it considerably more likely that we'll get the results we want. One communication method does not fit all.

When we start making generalisations, there are always going to be a few outliers. Here's where many people go wrong: Many reps start widening their message to try and be relevant to ten out of ten prospects. Resist this urge and instead think about how you could change your message so it will be a direct hit for six of the ten. The broader we make the message, in the hopes of hitting all ten, the less likely that we hit *any* of them between the eyes. This is a big problem because this lack of immediate relevance causes prospects to perceive our outreach as spam. We need to do better. We need to think about targeting prospects with the pinpoint accuracy of a sniper scope, not blasting away with a machine gun.

To do this, we need to grow comfortable with making some assumptions about our prospects based on what we absolutely know about them and people just like them. This is simpler than it sounds. With a bit of practise, we'll soon be doing it almost intuitively. Don't overthink it.

Smart Targeting Questions

- What do the last 10 clients you signed have in common?

- What problems drove your conversations with these prospects?

- How and in what channels did these prospects engage with you?

- What reasons did they give for engaging with you?

To start this process, create a mental picture of your prospect and then commit it to paper. You'll find an ICP (Ideal Client Profile) template in Appendix 2 that will help you get used to profiling your prospects before you ever talk to them. I suggest you use it. Revise it as many times as necessary until your description is so vivid a stranger could use it to ID your ideal prospects out of a police line-up.

More Outreach ≠ More Sales

There is no effective outreach without a clearly defined target market. When you know that the person on the other end of your outreach will be receptive to your specific compelling story, you'll be able to:

➡ Give your prospects a compelling reason to connect

➡ Move quickly towards high-quality conversations

➡ Customise your outreach faster

➡ Get high-quality referrals

➡ Make prospect lists quickly

Stop thinking good prospects are scarce, that they are hard to find, and that there are too few of them. This mindset holds you back from targeting smarter. How? People are desperate to obtain things that are considered scarce. If you're desperate to find your ideal client, you're more likely to be tempted to widen your selection criteria. Every adjust- ment wider makes it significantly harder for you to target effectively and harder for the prospect to believe you are talking to them directly. The wider you look the harder it is to engage.

Rather than focusing on the prospect and their particular problems, you'll end up positioning yourself as a commodity supplier (as expendable and replaceable as rolls of toilet paper).

What we want is the opportunity to present ourselves as trusted advisors—as scarce as hens' teeth and entirely irreplaceable. We solve very strategic problems, so we can command a much higher price. People who solve big, strategic problems get paid big money—it's really that simple. Miss this opportunity and you'll find yourself under steadily increasing pricing pressure. You'll be asked again and again to justify your prices until either you or they reach their breaking point.

When we target our outreach at prospects who will view us as something more than commodity suppliers, we'll start seeing the difference almost immediately. Smart targeting shows up as:

➜   Fewer cancelled meetings

➜   Less price-focused clients

➜   More second and third meetings

My clients usually come to me to solve a very specific problem. They need more pipeline and more sales conversations. I'm here to help them find more ideal clients and start conversations with them. Sure the vehicle we use to get that result might change. But I can count on one hand the number of times clients have walked into my office and asked me to overhaul their sales process from top to bottom. They come to me because they know I can help them build a pipeline full of great opportunities. My focus is on the front of the funnel, so I target people and businesses with problems in that specific area.

I can trace the bulk of my success to the fact that I've never tried to be all things to all people. I've never tried to adapt my message to make it fit my entire TAM (total addressable market). Instead, I've put a small corner of the market in my sights and aimed at my ideal customers, putting a bead right between their eyes. This has made all the difference.

Pillar 3: Smart Messaging

The quality of the message we send out to our ideal prospects and clients has a direct impact on whether they will reply to us or not. We need all five of the pillars of prospecting to be effective, but everything we've built will quickly crumble if our messages don't resonate with our prospects. The other four pillars are all about getting the message out and getting eyeballs on to it. This, on it's own, does not compel our prospects to take action. Only message quality can do that. This why we need to employ smart messaging.

Reps typically struggle with effective messaging because they lose sight of their prospects' commercial reality. Instead, they focus on the product and its features rather than the commercial benefits it delivers for the customer. Marketing paraphernalia tends to shape our messages, but we should not be taking marketing talking points directly to our prospects.

Let's say that you sell drills. The prospect you're talking to is a homeowner who wants to hang a picture in their living room, and they need a drill to sink the hook on which they will hang that picture. For this particular customer, a message that focuses on the quality of the drill or its features will be ineffective. A more effective message will be one that focuses on how nice the living room will look once the picture is hung. The homeowner doesn't want the drill; they don't want the hole in the wall; they don't want the hook in the hole; it's not even the painting on the wall they want. They want the *feeling* that looking at the picture on the wall will give them. Ask yourself, what result are you really selling to your clients?

When your messaging doesn't clearly align with the prospect's problem, you lose credibility, and once it's lost, it's never coming back. It's spam. We build credibility by making sure that our messaging is premised on a one-to-one relationship. Good messaging approaches conversations as one to one; spammy messaging is perceived as one to many.

> **Message quality is key**
> If you don't want to sound spooky or spammy, build out strong messaging that works in a tight niche.

Even a single spammy message can sink your battleship. If you're using LinkedIn for outreach (which you should be), that spammy message will stay in the message thread between you and your ideal prospect. Even if you change roles (or prospecting styles), that message is like a weight around your neck that you might never be able to shake off. Too many reps end up learning this the hard way.

The same goes for spooky messages (when a personalisation attempt hits too close to home for the prospect's comfort). There is an abundance of personal information readily available online if you know how to look for it. You can find out what school your prospect went to, what kind of car they drive, the names of their children and pets, and what they had for lunch. Bring these up in your outreach and you'll be barging into their private lives. You haven't earned the right to be this familiar yet—indeed, you may never earn this right. Spooky messages make the prospect feel like they've been stalked. Rather than endearing yourself to them, you're making their skin crawl. No one is going to engage in a conversation with a spooky stalker.

> Even if your feelings are hurt, never send **awkward break-up emails** to prospects. They never produce the desired effect.

When we get our message quality right, our words present us as a peer, a valuable resource, and a trusted advisor—not (and this is crucial) as a servant. It's true, reps need to bring results and, in order to do that, we often need to do much of the work to keep a transaction on schedule and alive, but this doesn't need to extend to the way we communicate and interact with our clients and prospects.

For example, if you are meeting with an executive for the first time and they ask you if you'd like a coffee or some water, instead of being polite and saying, "No, I'm fine", say, "Yes, that'd be great". Having them fetch you some water or getting you a coffee or tea signals that you are on the same social level as they are. Rather than positioning yourself as a servant, you're sending a clear message that the conversation you're about to have is as valuable to them as it is to you. If possible, walk with them to the kitchen and get the drinks together. This might make them more receptive to working together on something as peers.

Remember that your pre-meeting conversation is often just as important as the meeting itself. Forget tired topics like the weather or sports. Instead, show them you've done your homework. Ask them about a strategic aspect of their business. Try something like this:

> *"Hey Gary, in my preparation for this meeting, I read in the AFR that your business has grown its sales head count by 35 percent in just the last two years. I'm interested, is it difficult to find that many good sales people today? What's your secret?"*

Remember, we get delegated down to those we sound most like. Sound like a business consultant, not a commodity supplier, and you'll be treated like one. Focus on their challenges and business priorities not your products and services.

Pillar 4: Multi-Channel

The fourth pillar is the one that most sales reps have trouble wrapping their heads around. Having been tied to only a channel or two for most of their career in sales makes them reluctant to adopt a multi-channel approach. Making the change takes no small amount of courage, but when you start to see your response rates climbing northward, you'll wonder why it took you so long to catch up.

By reaching out to prospects across various channels, we dramatically increase the chances that we move out of their peripheral vision and into that space where we are awarded their full and undivided attention.

There are eight channels we'll want to look at. There are others, but these are the ones we'll be focusing on in this book:

➜   Phone

➜   Email

➜   Reply email

➜   Text

➜   Video

➜   Social

➜   Direct mail

➜   Inside help

The only one of these that might be new to you is inside help. This is where you look to your extended network to help you either make or confirm contact. Reaching out for help might mean talking to your boss, someone in your team, or someone in your network—anybody who can help you get the conversation started. If all other avenues seem closed, look for help (just like the team link function in LinkedIn SalesNAVIGATOR).

When we spread our outreach across multiple channels, we tend to get that deeper and genuine consideration we're after. The prospect might ignore or delete two or three of our touch attempts, but that doesn't matter. We will send enough of them across various channels to get through so that they get even just a few seconds of deliberate attention. So long as our message quality is high, even a few seconds of their attention is enough.

Research released by XANT in 2019 says that using a variety of channels in our outreach dramatically increases outreach effectiveness. When we use just one channel, 9.5 percent of our outreach is effective. When we use two, that number more than doubles to 22.5 percent. When we use three tools, it rises again to 25.1 percent.

XANT also found that the phone remains the outreach channel most commonly used by reps. The most common outbound cadence was a single phone call. This was used in 26.5 percent of all outreach. This highlights just how much single attempt sales activity is still happening. Having (and using) a follow-up sequence across various channels means you will be a leader in your industry. The bar is lower than you might think. Use as few as three or four channels for real cut through.

There is a widespread fear among reps that spreading their outreach into multiple channels simultaneously will lead to them coming across as desperate or spammy. Let me put that to bed. Consider the following:

➡ According to an Inside Sales report, sales outreach that uses two communication channels (as opposed to one) is 167 percent more effective. Outreach that uses three channels is a further 19 percent more effective.

➡ As recently as 2018, The Bridge Group reported that the best reps make 12 or more attempts to successfully engage with a prospect. More recent data suggests that times have changed. An effective outreach campaign can now start to expect successful results in as little as 4 attempts.

➡ According to sales experts Gabe Karson and AJ Hunt, reps make 75.2 percent fewer contact attempts than they think they do.

We've all received a call or email or two from a rep only to have the outreach stop when we don't respond immediately. This is typical prospecting. They don't switch channels. It's one and done. This is how most of us handle single-channel outreach. Unless it's a direct hit, right between the eyes with the first shot, we simply ignore it until it goes away. And it usually does go away.

Using a multi-channel strategy interrupts this pattern. If you've ever been approached with a multi-channel strategy, you know what I'm talking about. If an email arrives in my inbox, followed shortly by a social outreach on LinkedIn, a phone call with a voicemail, and, to top it all off, a personalised piece of mail lands on my desk, I'm intrigued. Something unusual is going on—unusual in a good way—and I'm intrigued. The rep clearly believes that what they have to share is of real importance to me.

I was recently approached by two marketing software suppliers simultaneously. The first one sent me a few emails on the day after I visited their website. The emails promised a follow-up call, and my phone rang the next day. Everything was as I expected it to be. I didn't answer the call, and that was the last I heard from them.

The second one took things further. There were a few emails and a phone call, but they added a degree of personalisation by also reaching out to me through LinkedIn. The interaction came from the same account rep who had called me, so it *felt* more urgent. The productive conversation that followed was the result of the rep's willingness to spread her outreach across multiple channels. She found that tipping point, and she found it quickly, creating a quick and meaningful engagement.

When multi-channel is done well, I'm forced to make a deliberate decision. Even if I take no immediate action, I have to make a fully conscious decision whether or not to engage with their outreach. I can't just reject them reflexively. This is crucial.

> **We need to earn our prospects' attention.
> Doing exactly what everybody else is doing will
> only take us so far. To outperform, we need to do
> what others won't do.**

A good multi-channel strategy disrupts expectations, building awareness and urgency as it spreads across channels. When we stop at one or two channels (like most reps), we are dramatically limiting the effectiveness of our outreach and probably wasting good leads.

When we spread out across channels, we are engaging with prospects in vastly different modes. An email will probably be read whilst they're at their desk (if it gets read at all); a text will get read within 90 seconds of its arrival; they might respond to a social interaction whilst in the lift; a video might get watched at home or when they are on a bus or a train. By spreading out our outreach, we're far more likely to catch them as they flip from one channel to another during the day.

Pillar 5: Sequence

The final pillar is when we establish a concrete sequence for our multi-channel outreach. We'll be looking at this in much more detail when we start building our cadence, but it's important that we do some preliminary thinking about how we'll be approaching our prospects.

We can't just fly by the seat of our pants. We've been doing this for years, and it doesn't work. We need a concrete sequence that nails us down to something—this is the only way we can keep ourselves accountable. Without a defined set of processes, we're just twisting in the wind.

> **Reps recall making 15 attempts to a prospect yet the data shows only 4. Reps tend to overestimate (often dramatically) the amount of outreach they conduct.**

The question you'll need to look at closely when you are building your cadence is what kind of sequence is most appropriate for your product and for your prospects. If you're dealing with a short buying cycle (office supplies, domestic freight, temp staffing, etc.), you might like to run a short cadence with a high attempt frequency. If you have a longer buying cycle (SaaS and other software solutions or government buyers), there might be an existing supply contract. Changing suppliers is something that can take months or years. This would mean a much longer cadence with a considerably lower frequency (perhaps 15 touches across 20 weeks).

If you're looking at these longer cadences, try to find a strategic time to start and stop. If, for instance, you happen to know that your prospect will be signing a new contract (either with the existing supplier or a new one) in 28 weeks, you can start a 16-week cadence that finishes, 12 weeks short of the contract renewal date. This way, you get the opportunity to engage well before the prospect is negotiating new contract terms with suppliers. You can be the voice in the back of their head telling them that there might be better options out there.

This is a great strategy because not many businesses have the rigour to start their renewal conversations 6 months before a 12-month contract renewal. You could easily find yourself in a high-quality conversations with potential clients who you know:

A. Currently use your products (or something similar)

B. Have a budget

C. Are in the buying window

These are the kinds of qualified leads that every rep wants in their pipeline. Prospects heading towards a new contract will be significantly more likely to engage with you than those who have recently signed a 12-month (or longer) contract. Whenever possible, align your prospecting sequence with dates like this. You'll find yourself having far more produc- tive and fast-moving conversations if your prospects have a defined change date.

When you are starting your cadence planning, populate with proven rhythms and durations to get started quickly. The ones that I've found successful in many situations are ones that see between 7 and 10 attempts across 8 weeks. If you're looking at a longer cadence, something in the range of 9 to 13 attempts across 12 weeks is an excellent place to start.

When we get our sequence right, our prospects know that we are *deliberately* trying to engage with *them* (as opposed to just any*body*) in a conversation.

Finding the right sequence is a delicate balancing act. If we go too slow, we don't get noticed. We can't build any pressure or urgency. If we go too fast, the prospect may not have had the opportunity to process the last piece of information before we start overwhelming them with more. For instance, when I download whitepapers, I often find that the SDRs call me before I've had a chance to read it. When this second touch happens too fast, you're telling your prospect that you don't understand them, their daily routines, or their buying behaviour.

> **"Instead of calling a prospect immediately after they download a whitepaper or infographic to see if they have any questions, simply ask if it downloaded ok."**
> —*Dean Mannix*

Taking time to think and plan out your cadence ahead of time takes all the pressure off both the reps and the sales leaders. Cooler heads prevail in these planning sessions and both parties can agree on the volumes, frequency and duration of outreach. This preplanning means there is less room for our 'sellers' bias' to impact reps later on and sales leaders can take some comfort knowing exactly what outreach will happen, when and how. Making decisions about what outreach and what channel to use 'on the fly' does not lead to optimal outcomes.

Too many reps lack this kind of clarity and consistency in their outreach. When I ask reps what they'll be doing this time next week, they often shrug their shoulders and offer little in the way of specifics. A surprising number of sales leaders have surrendered to this. They've effectively thrown up their hands and accepted this as the new reality.

> **Whilst reps overestimate the amount of outbound activity they have conducted against each prospect, prospects underestimate how much activity they have seen from each rep. There is a massive disconnect.**

It's the ostrich effect, and it's dragging down sales team performance across the board. One of the first things I ask new clients to provide is detailed data about their outreach sequencing. The companies that require only fine tuning are the ones that have extremely clear sequencing in place. The ones that need a complete overhaul are, without fail, the ones trying to hit their quotas with their heads in the sand.

In some sales departments, quotas are the *only* metric of any importance. Reps are left in charge of sequencing. Some hit the bullseye; many others miss the mark. With the use of a pre-determined cadence, reps have something easier to aim at—something they can hit repeatedly on the first try. When they find success earlier and easier with a prescribed sequence, they become far more likely to stay the course and find success. This success creates higher levels of rep confidence and motivation. When we tell them to hit their quota (and little else), they're aiming at something way out on the horizon. When we plan out a cadence together and show them what will get them to that target, it becomes achievable. We're asking them to take small steps, not over-whelming them by asking them to make one huge leap.

Sales leaders too love the process of mapping out their teams' sequences as it gives them confidence that there is an agreed level of outreach and follow-up taking place in a predetermined rhythm across predetermined and agreed channels. Micro-management strategies disappear. They're happier, and so are the reps they are managing.

Our sequencing will be determined by three factors:

1. Duration — How long will the outreach last (usually expressed in weeks)

2. Frequency — How often will we attempt to make contact (usually expressed in attempts per week)

3. Volume — How many times total will we attempt to make contact (duration multiplied by frequency)

Sequencing depends on our ability to assign precise values to each of these, and, whilst I can say that, typically, we should be aiming at a volume of between 7 to 10 attempts per prospect, this is a very broad guideline. Duration and frequency depend entirely on your specific prospects' personas, their buying cycle, and the number of barriers (gatekeepers etc.) you'll need to clear during your outreach. If the buying cycle is extremely short, your duration will be short as well. Generally, as duration rises, frequency falls and vice versa.

Sequencing is all about finding that sweet spot, and this means knowing when to apply prospecting pressure and when to abandon the pursuit (when further time spent pursuing simply becomes a wasted resource). Some outreach has a pre-determined endpoint. If, for instance, you are conducting a campaign around a limited time offer or an event, your outreach window will have a clearly defined frame. If there is no pre-determined endpoint, you'll want to assign some reasonable limits to your outreach. This means finding that tipping point (in both duration and frequency) when professional persistence tips into unprofessional pestering.

If you're dealing with a short buying cycle (usually a more transactional type of sale), a month of outreach is probably more reasonable. If the buying process is longer, or if multiple stakeholders are involved, you might be looking at an 8, 12, or 16-week campaign (sometimes even longer than this for enterprise or government acquisitions).

It's not always immediately apparent what number you should be aiming at, so it's often best to workshop duration questions with reps and sales leaders from your team who are selling in these markets now. If there's any difficulty coming to agreement, use the cadence templates that I've provided for you in this book. They're an excellent starting point that can be adjusted as you go along.

You'll notice that some of the cadence examples have higher duration and lower frequency than others. If you feel as though one of these examples is a perfect fit for you, by all means use this to build out your sequence, but I always suggest a little tweaking to make sure that you've plugged the right numbers into the equation.

Once you've determined the duration, all you need to do is prescribe the frequency of outreach. Is it more than once per week, once per week, or even less than this? The same rules I described above when talking about frequency also apply to duration. A more transactional sale with a faster buying cycle might be best influenced with twice-weekly attempts. If it's a longer and more strategic sales play, you might want to schedule outreach for every 10 to 12 days.

Knowing your duration and frequency will help you determine your volume. All you do is multiply duration by frequency to get your volume. For example, twice-weekly attempts for four weeks will give you a volume of eight attempts.

* * *

Of course, outreach specifics vary wildly, but these specifics sit on top of the five pillars I've outlined in this chapter. If you start with the right mindset, understand who is in your ideal market, craft your message smartly, use multiple channels to broadcast these messages, and then build a powerful sequence, you'll have a strong foundation that can and will support your outreach. The result will be more valuable sales conversations with your ideal clients.

Chapter 4
Increasing Your Influence

If we're going to create and send a message to a prospect with the goal of them taking some sort of action (e.g., calling us back, taking a meeting, attending an event, etc.), we need to approach this strategically. Inside our message, we need to use influential messaging strategies that are scientifically proven to increase the effectiveness of our requests.

Fortunately, we have a huge body of research and evidence that we can apply that helps us do exactly that. The theories that we'll be looking at in this chapter have over 70 years of behavioural science research supporting them. The science is clear, but still, the principles of persuasion that we'll be discussing in this chapter remain under-used and poorly understood in the sales sphere.

> **By applying the principles of influence to your outreach, you can increase your response rates by as much as 30 percent.**

I've spent so much of my career talking about the science of persuasion and the power of influence that I feel I could almost write an entire book on persuasion itself. However, since persuasive messages are only one part of the cadence, I'll merely provide a short overview of the theory. This should be enough to get started on your journey towards becoming a master persuader.

The 6 Universal Principles of Persuasion

Our lives are extremely busy. Every day, we make thousands of decisions. We can't give all of these decisions our full attention, so we subconsciously look for reliable shortcuts that can help us make those decisions easily and quickly.

In 1984, after a long period of extensive field research amongst sellers and influencers, Robert Cialdini published his award-winning book, *Influence: The Psychology of Persuasion*. In his book, Cialdini describes six universal principles that he says we all use to make these decision short-cuts, calling them the Six Principles of Persuasion.

In what follows, I'll break down these principles one and a time. What I find is that whenever I share these strategies, whether it be in workshops or with my private clients, there is always a sense of acknowledgement. Typically, people know these approaches are highly persuasive. Undeniably, the principles of persuasion pull us magnetically towards certain behaviours. We can feel them acting on us and see them acting on others, but we don't have names for them.

More importantly, we don't know how to implement them in a way that makes sense and drives good outcomes.

If we can better understand what the principles of persuasion are and how they work, we can leverage them in our business communication. They can become a reliable tool that, when used responsibly, dramatically increase our levels of influence, which will change how our prospects respond to us.

By leveraging the Six Principles of Persuasion, we'll be increasing the chances our prospects will say yes and decreasing the chances they will say no.

Persuasion Principle 1: Reciprocity

People feel obliged to return a favour after they have received one.

Ask anybody who has ever waited tables, and they'll tell you. Diners are more likely to provide a larger tip if they received a free mint or liqueur at the same time they receive the bill.

This becomes even more powerful when it is personalised. Researchers found that tips increased four-fold when the waiter singled out the diners for praise and gave them extra mints as a personalised thank you. This maximised the sense of obligation, leaning hard into the principle of reciprocity.

The key to leveraging reciprocity is being the first to give. For maximum effectiveness, make it appear valuable, make it timely, and make it personalised.

> **Reciprocity Reflection**
>
> *What have you got to give that could be perceived as valuable? What can you give that can be personalised and delivered to prospects in a timely manner?*

Persuasion Principle 2: Authority

People look to those they perceive to be experts to show them the way to act or think.

People dressed in a pilot's uniform are significantly more likely than those dressed in street clothes to be successful when asking strangers for change on the street. Authority (even when it's only *perceived* authority) is a powerful influencer. Book authors are typically considered experts in their field, even if only they and their editors have actually read their book. Saying, "She wrote the book on it" is simply another way of saying that she is an authority and therefore to be trusted.

It's for this same reason that professionals display their degrees in prominent locations. They are increasing and reinforcing their level of authority with their clients.

Third-party authority can also be a valuable and highly effective tool. If, for example, we display a picture of us standing next to a pre-eminent expert, or if we are hosting an event featuring a respected authority, some of their authority rubs off on us.

This kicks into high gear when the third-party expert praises us (this is why authors love to get quotes—even short ones—from big names on the covers of their books). If they're praising us or our work, we must be worth a second look. If you want an immediate authority boost, find ways to align yourself with outstanding experts in your field. It's difficult to overstate the degree to which this kind of association can boost your reputation as an authority.

> **Authority Reflection**
>
> *In what situations could you leverage third-party authority more effectively? How might you draw your prospects' attention to your good reputation?*

Persuasion Principle 3: Scarcity

People typically want more of what they cannot have. The newer something is, or the harder it is to obtain, the more people want it.

Uluru, also known as Ayers Rock, a popular climbing spot for Australian adventurers, had an average of 130 climbers a day until they announced that, as of October 2019, climbers would no longer be allowed. In the last weeks before the rock face closed, more than 400 people visited the rock each day—a more than 300 percent increase.

As I write this, we're in the middle of the Coronavirus pandemic. The minute it became clear that the virus would not be respecting borders, Australians started buying up all the toilet paper they could get their hands on. The scarcer it became, the more the hoarding accelerated. More than an actual scarcity, it was the *perception* of scarcity that drove these problematic buying behaviours.

We can use scarcity to make our messages more persuasive by highlighting a product's lack of availability or a limited time offer. If a certain specialist is only available on a certain date or at certain times, this can increase the desire of those wanting to gain access to those products or services.

> **Scarcity Reflection**
>
> *How can you build scarcity into your messaging? How can you make your products or services seem more in demand or more difficult to obtain?*

Persuasion Principle 4: Liking

People want to say yes to those who are similar to themselves.

People want to buy from people they like. They will occasionally hold their noses and buy from somebody they dislike, but only if they can't find what they need elsewhere.

The driving force of liking as a persuasion principle is the perception of similarity. People tend to like (and buy from) people who they identify with in some significant way.

Something as simple as taking five minutes for a bit of small talk about common interests before entering a negotiation has been proven to increase the chances of agreement from 55 percent of the time to 90 percent of the time.

The more similarities between us and our prospects that we can highlight, the closer we inch to a deal with that person or that organisation. Whenever possible, find and remind your prospects of these common links. Who are the people you both know? What are the associations, groups or organisations that you are both members of? Answering questions like these will make creating conversational engagement much easier.

> **Liking Reflection**
>
> *What opportunities do you have to highlight similarities between you and your prospects?*

Persuasion Principle 5: Consistency

People like their actions to be consistent with their public statements.

Nobody wants to look like a hypocrite. I want to be a man of my word, and I'm sure I can say the same of you.

This can be a powerful persuader. Researchers found that they had significantly more success persuading residents to place a large placard promoting safe neighbourhood driving on their front lawn when those same residents had previously placed a smaller sticker on their window pledging their support for safer speed limits. The small public statement opened the door to a much stronger commitment because the one was consistent with the other.

Applying consistency as a persuasion tactic in a sales situation might be as simple as asking those prospects who have agreed to a meeting with you to tell you why they agreed to meet. Dig deeper. Ask them why they thought you, specifically, will be able to help them solve a particular problem. When they answer, they will be making a statement about why they think your solution is a good fit for their problem. Later, they'll want to remain consistent with this statement.

> **Consistency Reflection**
>
> *How can you create a situation where your prospects freely announce a preference for you or your solution?*

Persuasion Principle 6: Social Proof

When deciding on a course of action, people take cues from groups with which they closely identify.

We certainly value our individuality, but the pull of the crowd is almost impossible to resist. The more closely we identify with the group, the more likely that we'll align our behaviour with that group.

Online retailers have become experts at the use of social proof. At the check-out, we often see pop ups: "People who bought this, also bought this...and this...and this..." Retailers who have adopted this social proof strategy have seen a significant rise in impulse sales.

When we are approaching our prospects, we can use social proof in subtle but effective ways. When we can show the prospect that people (crucially, people *like them*) have made the decision to trust us, we are showing them that we have numbers on our side—and there's safety in numbers.

> ### Social Proof Reflection
>
> *How can you highlight what others are doing so that your prospects feel as though engaging with you is the safe choice?*

* * *

Professionals who learn to entwine these six persuasive principles into their daily communication often see an impressive increase in request effectiveness. Best of all, these persuasive techniques work well across all communication platforms: social media, email, phone, and face-to-face.

When my clients ask me for just one sales strategy to work on, I tell them to work on the art of persuasion. "Out of all the different strategies I've learnt and taught across 25 years of selling and training," I say, "nothing makes a difference like persuasion." When they take my advice and apply the art of persuasion to their outreach, they see an almost immediate difference in how their prospects are responding. If you are looking for one key to sales success in this book, this is it.

A few final points: Persuasion should be an art that is always practiced ethically and legally. We need to make sure that we are fully compliant with whatever our industry says we are allowed or not allowed to say in our outreach. Make sure you comply with your organisation and your industry's specific compliance guidelines.

It almost goes without saying, but I'll say it anyway: We cannot lie to our prospects. We've worked hard to build up a good reputation, and we shouldn't be willing to take risks with it. Always remain genuine and authentic in your claims. Reputations take a long time to build, but they can be destroyed in an instant.

Finally, avoid the overlapping influence trap that so many fall into. Don't cram your messages full of influence strategies. This is not going to supercharge your results. The most persuasive messages typically lean into one or two principles of persuasion. Any more than this and it'll become obvious what you're doing. Persuasion is undoubtedly a less is more scenario.

When you review the templates I've provided for you in the appendices, you will see that all messaging contains a persuasion principle, but rarely more than one or two of them.

Chapter 5
The Cadence

The cadence features a series of touches strategically placed across multiple communication channels over a defined period. When consistently and patiently applied, it dramatically increases prospect reply rates and lead qualification.

It works because it builds first awareness and then intrigue with our prospects, providing several opportunities for them to interact with us. This leads reliably to collaborative communication with the prospect. We grab their attention and, eventually, they give us access to their calendars.

Because we take a longer view with a planned and deliberate cadence we don't need the prospect to engage with us the very first time. We have the ability to structure a more complex story across several outreaches, this provides opportunities for our messaging to be more educational— never needy or desperate. Gary Vaynerchuk calls this the jab, jab, jab, right hook, and it's a knockout technique like no other. The concept is simple: three jabs of value in your comms followed by the right hook (your ask). Our cadence programming is built on a similar combo strategy.

Non-cadence strategies typically consist of only one or two outreaches, and usually in only one or two channels. They start swinging at the first bell, asking early and pushing hard for that quick knockout. They are easy to ignore because they look and sound like every other piece of dismissible outreach. When we apply a disciplined approach, with multiple messages across multiple channels, our outreach stands out from the crowd. It produces a deeper engagement, which tips the battle for a response in our favour.

When I introduce the cadence to reps, many of them tell me that they're already using a cadence in their prospecting efforts (they just aren't *calling* it a cadence). They are, they say, already reaching out to their prospects at regular intervals, and they're communicating via a number of different channels and trying to start conversations in a number of different ways.

I ask for more details: "What kind of process are you using?" I'll ask. What they describe is often the very opposite of a process. It's ad hoc and undisciplined, a mashup of half-baked ideas, vaguely defined theories, and loose strategies. There is no consistency, no coherent set of principles and plans. They're flying by the seat of their pants, making it up as they go along. There's no system, so there's no ability to replicate successful outreach programs and eliminate the unsuccessful ones.

Even if they are finding some success with their outreach, it's up and down. When I ask them why they do something in a particular way, they lean on hunches or talk about finding occasional success through trial and error.

This is not a cadence.

Cadence Components

A cadence has a number of components which, when placed together, create a concerted and effective outbound methodology. Since each moving part interacts with all of the others, if we remove even one of the components, the machine breaks down.

We're going to be building our cadences out of six components:

1. Touches

2. Channels

3. Attempts

4. Duration

5. Frequency

6. Content

When we start building our cadence, we'll be assigning definite quantitative values to each of the cadence components. There's a very good reason for this. Sales reps have a tendency to overestimate (often dramatically) how much outreach they conduct. According to 2019 XANT data, reps over-report outbound touches by a ratio of as much as three to one.

My own experience confirms this. When reps report that they are reaching out to a prospect between 9 to 15 times, the actual number is usually closer 4. Reps aren't being deceptive. They are just allowing themselves to be guided by perceptions rather than reality, and this means lots of outreach ends up falling by the wayside. Sellers' bias strikes again.

The lack of clarity surrounding what is actually getting done can make it almost impossible to gauge the success or failure of our outreach. It only becomes a cadence when there is discipline and consistency—we need to do *exactly* what we say we're going to do. We can't stop when we *feel* like we've done enough. Chances are we haven't done nearly enough. The cadence enforces discipline and predictability in our outreach. It tells us when we should quit and when to keep persisting.

> **Discipline: Doing the right things at the right time— every time.**

When we start applying this disciplined approach to outreach, we'll be making better use of our prospecting time, increasing our response rates, and making our outbound truly measurable and then scalable. By taking the guess work out of outreach, we can make sure that reps have at their disposal a process that they and their managers know works. The result is increased performance across the board.

Let's take a closer look at each of the six components of the cadence.

Touches

A touch is an outreach via any one of the channels we'll be discussing below. A phone call is a touch; so is an email, a social media outreach (mostly via LinkedIn or Twitter), a text message, or a piece of direct mail. Recently, video messaging (delivered via text or email) has become an effective form of outreach, so if you're using video messaging to communicate with your prospects, this counts as a touch as well. We also have my personal favourite: the help touch. We'll return to all of these later.

> **When is a touch a touch?**
> To qualify as a touch we don't need to speak to a prospect. A call without an answer is a touch. An email without a reply is also a touch. By being consistent and combining touches, we create sustained prospecting pressure.

Channels

Each touch is carried out via a channel. These are the eight channels we use:

- Phone
- Text
- Email
- Reply email
- Social
- Direct mail
- Video
- Help

You're almost certainly familiar with seven of these, but one of them (help) might need a little explaining. Using the help channel means asking for help from someone either within your organisation or your network. This might mean asking your sales manager to help you connect with your prospect's boss, or it might mean having somebody in your office send your prospect a message suggesting that you and they connect on LinkedIn.

The connection doesn't have to be in your office. You might share a supplier or a customer. Leverage these common connections. Asking for help will get easier the more often you do it (provided that you're not always going to the same well for water). Nothing helps accelerate a cadence like help.

Attempts

Each time we reach out to a prospect, we are making an attempt, but an attempt is not the same as a touch. An attempt is comprised of multiple touches. These touches happen in quick succession, spreading across multiple channels. An email, a voicemail, and a text together would comprise an attempt; so might a connection request, a piece of direct mail, and a phone call. What channels you use will depend on your prospects and their communication preferences (we'll return to this below).

The goal of a touch and an attempt is the same (to make contact with a prospect), but we increase the possibility that the latter will be successful by making sure that every attempt (without fail) is comprised of multiple touches.

Duration

Duration measures the amount of time you spend deliberately pursuing a prospect. The duration determines how long it will be before you move on (i.e., stop pursuing a prospect). In a more transactional type of selling situation, three or four weeks might be long enough. If you're selling to large corporations or to the government sector, duration might stretch for months or even longer than this. Generally, the higher the dollar figure attached to your product, the longer the duration and (usually) the lower the frequency.

Earlier in this process, you did some thinking about who your ideal clients are. We can work outwards from there to gain at least a provisional understanding of their preferred communication tools, their decision-making process, and the response times you can expect.

When building your cadence, it's wise to treat duration as tentative. You might find more success by moving from an eight-week duration to a ten-week one, or you might reduce time wasted on unresponsive prospects by making your cadence a little shorter. You'll know when you've hit the duration sweet spot after you've run a few cadences.

Frequency

Frequency means how many attempts we are making per week or per month. With short, transactional buying cycles, you should be making multiple attempts per week. A larger, slower-moving sales situation might mean only two or three attempts per month.

Higher frequencies work very well in B2C selling situations or with inbound leads. A more strategic B2B buying journey usually has a lower frequency, with perhaps as much as a few weeks elapsing between attempts. It will depend entirely upon your prospect's role and the industry they work in. If, for instance, you're selling to a head of sales, frequency will probably be high. If you're selling to the marketing or HR department, frequency will probably be lower.

The key to frequency is adopting a rhythm, which means keeping in lock step with your plan. If you've decided on a one attempt per week frequency, that attempt needs to happen every week like clockwork. It doesn't have to happen at the same time (it's actually better if we mix this up a bit), but it does have to happen *every* week without fail. Miss a beat and you'll risk missing your chance.

Content

Content is not limited to the emails we send or the scripts we use when phoning our prospects. Content includes what we attach to those emails or what we ask permission to send during those calls. When we make this request, we are asking the prospect to give us their time, so we need to make the time investment worthwhile for them.

Content might include any of the following:

➜ Authored articles (excellent if you're trying to establish yourself as an expert)

➜ Third-party articles (either by members of your organisation or others of note)

➜ Whitepapers on industry information

➜ Reports on relevant industry trends

➜ Books

➜ Industry news (the more relevant, the better)

➜ Event invitations (industry events not just yours)

➜   Links to social content (use discretion)

➜   Video content (personalised is a great strategy)

➜   Infographics

Content is more important than ever. The right content at just the right time interrupts your prospects' pattern of thinking, disturbing their status quo by forcing them to question something they've previously taken for granted. We can either ask these questions directly, or (even better) we can frame content in such a way that it guides the prospect more gently towards asking these questions themselves with us as their guide to a better future.

> **"Questions create conversations, conversations build relationships, relationships become opportunities, and opportunities create sales."**
> —*Phil M. Jones*

Remember, if you're sending a long-winded report or article, be conscious of the time they will need to review and absorb the information. If a piece of content seems long to you, but you feel that the information it contains is crucial, still send it, but make sure to include a punchy summary of the important points. The aim is to provide value to the reader not overwhelm them with more reading material.

This is where it is most important to hit our prospects

between the eyes. The right piece of content adds gravitas to our outreach. An ill-considered piece of content makes us seem frivolous. If you are remotely uncertain about whether a piece of content will land with a splash or a thud, keep it in hand until you're sure that it will produce the desired effect.

As they say, wait until you can see the whites of their eyes before you fire your best shot.

Chapter 6
Prospecting Time Management

"I don't have time to prospect."

I regularly hear this from reps at all levels. Reps push prospecting further and further down their list of priorities until they no can longer find the time to prospect (at least not effectively). But prospecting is not something you should be *finding* the time for; it's something you need to *make* the time for. I guarantee, build this into a habit and this time will be one of the best decisions you'll make as a rep.

You can't afford to *not* make this investment of time and energy. If you continue to put prospecting off as something you'll get to when you find the time, you'll be choking off the lifeblood of your pipeline. Without the active inflow of new, high-quality prospects that a strong system of outreach can produce, you will soon find yourself talking to fewer and fewer quality leads. You'll end up desperate, striking up conversations with anybody who can fog a mirror, or (even worse) with no leads at all. You'll be left sitting on your hands waiting for the phone to ring.

Without regular prospecting, you'll risk talking to so few prospects that, when you eventually do get one on the line, your heart will be pounding in your chest and your palms will be sweating. You'll be desperate to make the sale, and few things are worse than a desperate sales rep. Desperate sales reps make terrible decisions and almost never say the right things.

> **Don't be a desperate seller.**
> **Nothing smells worse than commission breath.**

All of this can be avoided when we deliberately set aside time for prospecting, and this means *blocking it in*.

Block it In

Where does time management start? With our calendar. This is where we can make a plan concrete, where we can *make* the time to create opportunities rather than waiting for them to come to us.

Consider the vital importance of outreach. There's no success without new business, so you'd think that most reps would be making and implementing a plan for building and maintaining a strong and healthy pipeline. This isn't what we're seeing, though. Reps simply don't spend enough time building this out.

How much time do you think you should be spending on outreach per week? With the right tools and strategies, most reps can be successful with only 90 to 180 minutes of prospecting time per week. This is enough to establish a strong outbound cadence that will fill your pipeline.

Take Action: Block in 120 minutes per week for the next three weeks. Don't make a mental note to do this later. Do it now.

When you're blocking things in, remember that it is far more effective to schedule prospecting time across several days than it is to lump it all together into a single afternoon. One hour twice a week tends to produce better outcomes than one two-hour block.

A cadence works because it applies the right amount of pressure across multiple channels, which builds urgency quickly. Having a dependable rhythm is important, but we don't want to let the rhythm become monotonous. If you do all of your prospecting at the same time every single week, your outreach becomes too predictable. You're touching your prospects at the same location and in the same mindset every time.

The most effective reps build variety into their cadences. Being unpredictable in times, channels and frequency creates stronger response rates. Best practice is to block out various times across the week and to have these times vary from week to week.

For best results, when choosing your prospecting time, choose a few times when you think your prospects are likely to be receptive. If you've been smart targeting, you should have some idea what your ideal client's typical daily and weekly rhythms look like.

For years, my prospects worked in the event, entertainment and hospitality industry. I found that my prospects were late starters. Contacting them before 10:00 was a quick way to get barked at; 11:00 seemed to be the sweet spot. I also found that Tuesdays and Wednesdays were the days they tended to dedicate to admin, so I would call and push for appointments on these days, knowing that these were the times they would be most receptive to my request.

Later in my career, my prospects worked in the financial services sector. Again, it took some time to find the sweet spot. The times around the opening and closing of the local stock market were essentially no-fly time zones. Each industry has its own preferred time to talk turkey with vendors. Work together with your team to pinpoint these times and focus on them when you're blocking in your prospecting time.

Narrowing it Down

I know you want specific details on when is the *best* time to reach prospects—all reps want to find that sweet spot, and I am asked this question endlessly. I tell my clients that the best we can do is make an educated guess. Don't worry too much about the times. It's better to just get out there and start running your cadence without getting too nitpicky about when to schedule your attempts.

Below, I've provided you with the outreach schedules that have worked for me. These might be a good starting point, but you might find that entirely different days and times work better for you.

Days of the Week

➜ Across industries, the middle of the week (Tuesday, Wednesday and Thursday) tends to be prime prospecting time. With the right approach, Fridays can also be very good, but, no matter how good your outreach is, Mondays are generally the weakest.

Times

➜ Emails

  → Landing just before 16:00 on Tuesdays, Wednesdays and Thursdays

  → Transactional emails: 14:00-17:00 on Sunday afternoons

  → Strategic emails: 08:00-11:00 on Saturday morning (executives tend to be in strategic thinking mode early in the weekend, moving into more transactional modes as the weekend winds to its close)

➜ Calls

→ 08:30-09:15 and 14:30-18:30 every weekday except Monday (Friday afternoons are my favourite phone prospecting times)

➜ Social

→ 07:30-09:00 Tuesday-Thursday mornings

→ 18:00-21:00 Monday and Tuesday evenings

Finding the sweet spot is important, but don't place too much emphasis on it. Use the Nike slogan as a guide: Just Do It. Perfect timing isn't everything. It's a nice to have, and using the times above as a guideline will improve results, but it's better to prospect when you have the time available than to wait for the perfect time and then risk ending up doing nothing.

Now might be a good time to have a chat with your line manager about allocating some non-negotiable prospecting time each week across a number of days. If you manage these conversations with your manager correctly, this should make it less likely that you get dragged into those last-minute 'urgent' meetings or discussions that have little or nothing to do with helping you hit your quota.

I cannot emphasise this enough: consistency is the linchpin of the cadence. Manage your time carefully so that you *never* miss a set of sequences. Let a sequence or two pass you by without action and you'll be right back where you started.

Breaking it Down Minute by Minute

How much time do you really need to prospect? Less than you think. An attempt should only take you five minutes.

NEWS FLASH
An attempt only takes five minutes.

The problem is that most reps are spending too much of their time on other activities. According to a 2019 CSO Insights sales performance study, sales reps only spend an average of 30 percent of their time selling. The amount of time they spend on prospecting is only a small percentage of this selling time. If we can increase this number (and use our prospecting time wisely), we can start blowing through our quotas with ease.

Let's say that you have two hours of prospecting time per week. This works out to about 5 percent of most people's total working week, so it's very achievable. Two hours means 120 minutes of prospecting time. Since an attempt only takes five minutes, we can make as many as 24 attempts per week. If we round that down to allow a little bit of a buffer for distractions, we're left with a capacity of 20 prospects that we can work on any given week—assuming that we're making one attempt per prospect per week.

If you're running a higher attempt frequency, this means you will need fewer prospects in your pipeline. If, for instance, you're scheduling attempts at a frequency of twice per week (assuming the same two hours of prospecting time per week), you'll only need around 10 to 12 prospects in the front of your pipeline at a time.

This might not sound like enough prospects. I know a lot of sellers have well over fifty prospects in their pipeline at a time. Some have well over a hundred. Here's the problem with that approach. These sellers aren't actively pursuing the prospects in their pipeline—not unless they're spending 20 or 30 percent of their total work time prospecting.

> **Better to have a few too few prospects in your pipeline than a few too many. Most struggling reps have too many prospects in their pipeline —not too few.**

Most prospects in these crammed pipelines just sit in a holding pattern. They're just a name and company listing in a CRM. There isn't a strategy to engage them in a meaningful way. The whole purpose of a cadence is to spend our time in the right ways on the right prospects. We focus on a smaller number of prospects, and we move them towards meaningful and productive conversations much more quickly than we would without the cadence. It means fewer leads at the pipeline entrance but more qualified leads in the middle and at the end of our pipeline (where the good stuff happens). Using our time to concentrate on a smaller number of prospects might feel counterintuitive, but it is the best way to boost our conversation attainment ratio whilst not wasting leads.

If you bundle your prospects into very narrow target markets (which we'll be looking at in the next chapter), you'll be able to further accelerate your outreach. Your per attempt time might drop as low as three or four minutes. This is because the level of personalisation and customisation required per outreach can be much lower when your prospects share business challenges, personas, and communication preferences.

Managing Your Marketing Requirements

According to a 2019 CSO Insights report, most reps spend around 30 percent of their time on marketing activities (about as much time as they spend on selling). How can we manage the content part of the outreach process whilst still making time for prospecting?

I've helped teams build out effective cadences that leave more than enough time for their marketing activities. I do this by ramping them up from 90 minutes of prospecting activity per week to 240 minutes per week. We do this slowly, increasing gradually over 7 weeks. This allows us to maintain a balance of prospecting and marketing activities. We can build volume and momentum into our pipeline immediately whilst, at the same time, building our marketing content. Not having content and resources at the ready is an obstacle for many reps and their teams. Using a cadence helps us overcome this challenge.

In the cadence example below, the first two weeks contains only 30 minutes of prospecting time and 60 minutes for content preparation. Starting on the third week, we add 30 minutes per week until we peak at 240 minutes of prospecting and preparation time in weeks 7 to 9. By this point in the cadence, all of our content preparation work is done, and we can focus entirely on prospecting, creating pipeline, and starting great client conversations.

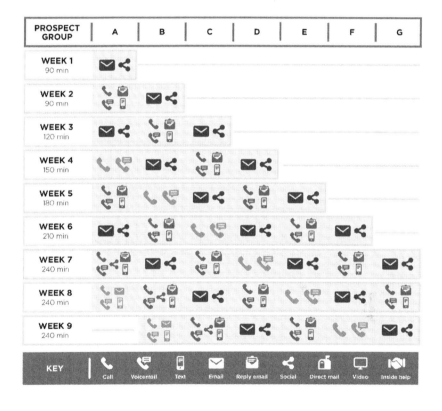

This kind of ramping up leaves us plenty of time early in the cadence to build out our content. We'll be doing this with the aid of the templates that I've provided in the appendices.

Building content creation into a ramped-up cadence like this keeps you ahead of your content requirements (rather than struggling to keep up or falling behind, which is where most reps find themselves). At the beginning of the cadence, whilst your prospect count is still low, we have time on our hands, and we can use that time to build our content, which we'll be using in the weeks ahead. Building it in advance results in much higher quality outreach. It is unrushed and deliberate, which is never the case when we prepare our content just in the nick of time.

Refer to the chart above. In week one, after you've sent your emails and reached out through your social channels, spend the remaining time building out the next week's touches. Specifically, in the above example, this means preparing your phone script, voicemail script, text message script, and your reply email #1 response. Examples and templates of all these and other outreach styles are available in the appendices. Remember, once you've created the content, you'll be able to re-use it in the following weeks. You'll only ever need to build it out the once.

This cadence example I've provided uses a frequency of one attempt per week per prospect. All attempts are multi-channel as you would expect. The time required to take action per prospect is only five minutes, regardless of the touch count or the channels used. We can keep this number low because we prepare our outreach the week before we use it.

Remember, this is just an example cadence that shows you one possible way of building out your cadence. Your own cadence will likely have different touch-channels, different durations, and different frequency. The process remains the same. You can adjust the variables to suit your selling style, industry, and buyer types.

Chapter 7
Build Your Own Cadence

I n this chapter, we use a standard eight-week, eight-attempt cadence to show you how to build out your prospecting plan in simple terms. You'll notice that there are nine weeks in this chapter. This is to help you see how the cadence extends as new prospects are fed into the system. In this model, each prospect gets eight weeks of prospecting time and eight attempts, but your prospecting continues indefinitely as prospects move in and out of your pipeline.

If you've decided you need a cadence that uses other variations of frequency, duration and touch types, adjust this model accordingly. Use the one that you think will provide best results, and if you think results could be better, make adjustments until you feel you're getting the absolute most out of your cadence.

Over the next nine weeks, step by step, week by week, you will be building a strong cadence that will substantially improve your outreach results. You'll be adding five new prospects every week, feeding them into the front of your cadence and engaging with them using multiple channels. With each engagement, you'll be moving them through your sequence. Until you're nearing the end of the cadence, you'll have time set aside every week to build out the content you'll be using during the following week's outreach.

> **The #1 Challenge for Sellers**
> **"Reps aren't talking to enough people**
> **enough of the time."**
> *—Dean Mannix*

Eventually, you will have all 45 prospects spread across all the various stages of your cadence. You'll be having meaningful conversations with many of them, and you'll have all the supporting marketing content that you'll need.

Being deliberate and measuring your progress and results will ensure that you're not wasting any of your precious leads. Your content will be on point, personalised, and unrushed. Because you've prepared ahead of time (rather than on the fly), you'll find your comfort and confidence growing with each call. Meeting your prospecting obligations (and your quota) will simply be a matter of following the plan.

Because the process is broken down week by week, we can look at each week in detail. This is what we'll be doing in this chapter. The complete nine-week cadence appears below. I've chosen a typical nine-week cadence, but cadences are most effective when they are customised. Yours might look a little different than the one we cover in this chapter. Remember that you can tweak this as much or as little as necessary until you find the right rhythm for you and for your prospects.

Standard 9 Week Cadence

Now, let's break this cadence down week by week.

In order to make it easier for us to see and understand what is happening in each week of the cadence. I've allocated five prospects each week to an alphabetical indicator. We'll call the first group of five prospects our Group A, the second we will call our Group B, the third Group C, so on until we reach the ninth week (Group I).

Week 1

Group A Email: We're going to start with an email. During the time set aside for content creation, use the introduction email template I've provided in the appendices. Personalise it based on the ICP you've prepared (also available in the appendices). The appropriate level of personalisation will depend on how much difference there is between the five prospects you've chosen. Personalisation and contextualisation should only take you a few extra minutes per touch.

Group A Social: After we've sent the first email, we move on to a simple social touch. This might mean something as non-invasive as viewing their LinkedIn profile, which means we pop up in their notifications. Because we've combined our social with our email, they will be more likely to view our profile in return. Assuming our profile is well configured to be truly compelling to the buyer, this creates a nice touch that supports our earlier email outreach.

We can dial up the intensity a bit by sending the prospect a connection request, or we can dial it up even further by liking some of their content, commenting on one of their posts, or interacting with some of their other social activity.

Make sure that your social interactions are on message with the email you sent earlier. At this early stage of the cadence, it's all about building awareness with the prospect, and we want to make sure that everything they notice displays consistency. If we spread our topics too broadly, we reduce the likelihood that they will connect the email to the social outreach. We want this connection to be obvious. Remember Vaynerchuk's jab, jab, jab, right hook knockout strategy? These early touches are the jabs.

If you do send a connection request, ensure it is person-alised. Highlight that the connection is for *their* benefit, not yours.

You should have plenty of time left over at the end of the week. Spend that time building out your week two content, adding personal touches wherever possible and appropriate.

Week 2

Group B Email: In week two, we add five new prospects into the pipeline. As in week one, we send each of them an introductory email, personalising and contextualising the content for maximum effect.

Group B Social: As in week one, we visit their LinkedIn profile. We might also want to like, comment, or otherwise engage with their social persona.

Group A Phone Call / Voicemail: We place a phone call to the prospect. If our email and social outreach were effective, we might get through, but it's just as likely that we end up leaving a voicemail. You'll find scripts for both of these in the appendices.

Be sure to log your prospects' names and numbers in your mobile. The last thing you want is to hum and haw whilst you're trying to remember who they are and where they are in your outreach. Make it easy on yourself by including their group (A, B, C, etc.) after their name in your contact file.

Group A Text: Immediately following the phone call/voice-mail, send the prospect a text (there's a template for this in the appendices).

Group A Reply Email: Finally, reply to your first email (check the appendices for an example). The timing is crucial here. Tony J. Hughes, author of *Combo Prospecting*, says that attempts should happen practically simultaneously. Phone call, voicemail, text, reply email—all inside a two-minute window.

Week two will see you making a total of ten attempts: five for the Group A and five for Group B. You will have some time left over for week three content preparation. Looking ahead, that means you'll be preparing a content-oriented email and another social interaction.

Week 3

Group C Email: The same introductory email that we've already sent to our A and B groups we now send to our C group.

Group C: Social: Same initial social activity as the two previous groups.

Group B: Phone Call / Voicemail: This is the second week of outreach for our B group, so now is the time to pick up the phone and call them, using the same approach that we used last week with the A group.

B Group: Text: Same as above.

B: Reply Email: Same as above. Remember that the voicemail, text, and email should all come through within around two minutes.

Group A: Social: We're changing gears with our social outreach in week three. Post an article and tag them or share a relevant post with them. The post or article needs to support the conversation you're trying to have with the buyer. For example, if you're trying to start a conversation centred on the macro-environment of an aging population, find some content that speaks *directly* about that topic and supports your message (in this case, perhaps something on how the weight of the aging population might impact the workforce distribution in the next few years as more and more people transition to retirement). Either tag them in the post or share it with them directly. Make sure you tell them why you think this is specifically relevant to them.

Group A: Email #2: We're also going to change up our email approach by sending them a content email (see template in appendices). The content email might include the same article or post that you shared with them elsewhere. This is often more effective than sharing multiple articles across multiple channels. Don't send too many different pieces of information to prospects too early. Remember, we are just trying to start a conversation at this point. We need to make it easy for them to engage. Better to focus on a single piece of content than to overwhelm them.

We're making 15 attempts this week (five for our A's, five for our B's, and another five for our C's). This will still leave you time to build out week four's content (you'll need a phone and voicemail script, and you'll need new personalised content for your A's). The phone script will be identical, because you haven't spoken to them yet. The voicemail script will need a slight adjustment to make it a little more familiar and to build on our outreach to date.

> **Never ask for a call back when leaving a voicemail. It sounds needy. Instead, tell them what you're going to do next: "I'll call you again in three days."**

Week 4

At this point in the cadence, our outreach begins to become a matter of maintaining consistency. Our A group is now at week four, and we carry on with another call and a voice-mail. All the other groups are covering the same ground that we've already covered with our A group. Our B group is at week three, getting the social outreach and the second email, and our C group is at week two getting the phone call/voicemail, text, and reply email.

We are introducing a new group of prospects (our Group D), and we'll need to spend a little bit of extra time personalising our outreach. Even with our growing number of attempts, there will still be time left over at the end of the week to build out next week's content.

If you work for a large organisation with a marketing department that supplies you with all of your content, this doesn't mean you need less time for content preparation. Spend your content time finding ways to personalise it for your prospects, making sure it always hits them right between the eyes.

How to Manage Replies

We've reached the half-way mark in our cadence, and I want to pause here for a moment to talk about managing replies. Perhaps as early as week one or two, some of your prospects will start responding to your outreach. Some will ask for more information, others will ask to be removed from further communication. We're beginning to have conversations with our prospects, and we need to manage these conversations carefully.

Let's start with the negative replies. When prospects opt out, there are a few things we can do. Usually, we feed them out of our cadence and into marketing's funnel (where they can be nurtured further). If the *no* is firm and final, we might mark them as 'do not contact' in our database. In most cases, though, the best response is to ask for permission to reach out again down the road. Suggest a specific time (six months often works) and then log that follow-up in your CRM. They can be fed back into your cadence at the appropriate time.

When the time comes to follow-up with these prospects, don't send them the same introductory email you send to fresh prospects. Reference your first communication, and remind them that, six months ago, you agreed to talk again in six months.

Now let's turn to the positive responses. You'll either hand the prospect over to an account executive (if you have a multi-tiered sales function), or you'll handle these prospect meetings yourself. Either way, the prospect is entering a new stage. Crucially, they are exiting your cadence. Every time we get a clear *yes* or a chance to explore things further with a prospect, they become an opportunity. Your prospecting activity only covers the top of your pipeline.

Every reply, positive or negative, translates to five minutes returned for us for the duration of the cadence. If one of our Group A prospects opts to take a meeting at week four, we no longer have five prospects in that group, only four. This reduces prospecting time pressure.

I find that, when I arrive at the end of my cadence, I've moved more than half of my prospects either out of the cadence or deeper into the pipeline. As a result, we can move through the later stages of the cadence quite quickly. We do the heaviest lifting in the first few weeks.

Week 5

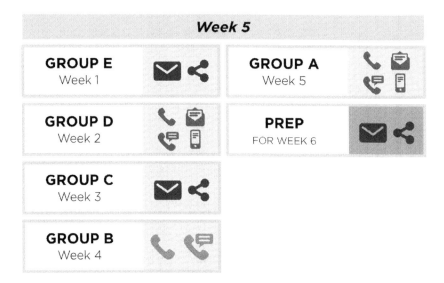

During week five, we add five new prospects (Group E), sending them our introductory email and making our first social touches. Our A's are now receiving a phone call/voicemail, a text, and we send them another reply email (this time, we are replying to the content email that we sent them two weeks ago).

Our B's get a phone call and a voicemail. Group C is one

week behind this, and our D's are just starting their second week.

If none of our prospects have opted out or in (highly unlikely at this stage), we have 25 prospects in our cadence at this point. This means a max of 125 minutes of prospecting time (25 prospects x 5 minutes per attempt). This leaves us with plenty of time to work on next week's content.

Week 6

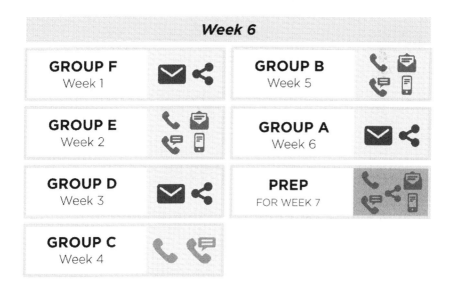

We now add our Group F prospects to our cadence. Our B's are now on week five, the C's are on week four, Group D is moving through week three, and Group E is starting its week two outreach.

Your A's have now spent a full five weeks in your cadence. During week six you'll be sending them a second content email (your third email, not counting your reply emails). Add emphasis here by focusing on how this content is particularly relevant for them. You'll also be supporting this with some new social activity (we'll be looking at this in more detail in the next chapter).

At this stage, your prospects (and especially your A's and B's) will almost certainly know that we are deliberately trying to start a conversation. If you've been using the smarter message guidelines, they've been receiving clear and persuasive messages, so you should be starting to get some responses.

As far as the social interaction is concerned, if you have not yet asked for a connection via LinkedIn, this would be a great time to do so. Leverage a common connection, highlighting your connections who share similar industry roles with your prospect. This helps build a peer-to-peer orientation—far more effective than the subservient sales rep chasing a sale orientation.

With the time you have remaining, continue to focus on building new personalised content for next week. Next week, you'll need a phone call, a new text message, a new voicemail, a new social interaction, and a new reply email that mentions the content email you sent last week.

Week 7

When we start week seven, 30 of our 45 prospects are in our cadence, and we're about to add five more. By this stage, somewhere between 30 and 60 percent of our prospects will have either opted in or out, clearing considerable room in our cadence. We're on the home stretch now. Let's jump in.

Our new group (our G's) are on their first week. Our remaining A's, who have been in our cadence for six full weeks now, are going to get our most aggressive attempt yet this week. We're going to reach out for some social interaction, then we're going to call them (leaving a voicemail if we don't get through). We'll also be texting them and replying to the content email that we sent last week.

We'll still be using the original script for the call to our remaining A's, but we'll be trying a different voicemail this time. We'll be building a message of scarcity by indicating that we'll

109

only be reaching out once more and that there is a specific reason they should talk to us. The text and the reply email will drive home a similar message (that the content we have shared with them can impact their business/operations). The social interaction should support the overarching messaging you have been presenting on other channels, or it should be trying to create some sense of obligation.

At absolute most, we have 35 prospects in our pipeline. This means 2 hours and 55 minutes of prospecting time (probably substantially less than this when we subtract those who have opted out or in). We can use our remaining time to prepare some of our closing touches. These have a slightly different message, so we'll need to prepare a new email, voicemail, and text scripts.

Week 8

We'll be feeding five new prospects (our H's) into the top of our cadence. They'll be starting the process just like everybody else: with a friendly social interaction and an introductory email.

The hardwearing A's are on their last week of attempts. During this last attempt, we change our language to create some urgency and scarcity. We call one last time. If unsuccessful, we leave a message acknowledging that, although the time may not have been right to chat, there is still value in chatting at some point. Then we tell them what we'll do: "I'll call you again in six months" or "I'll add you to our marketing list"—whatever you feel the appropriate next step is.

Your email and text message should take the same tone. You'll find some examples for all of these in the appendices.

All of the other groups are rolling from one week to the next. There's an overview of where all the groups should be at the end of the cadence on the next page.

You probably have your hands full with outreach and conversations with prospects at this stage, but there's good news: you don't need to create any more marketing content. You'll have a busy week of outreach, but you'll no longer have to balance this with content creation. With 40 prospects in your cadence, you'd be spending 3 hours and 20 minutes on outreach this week, but realistically you're probably looking at 2 hours and 30 minutes—perhaps less depending on your response rates.

Week 9

You should know the drill by now, but there's a lot of over-lapping prospecting at this stage, so let's look at how our groups are presenting more broadly:

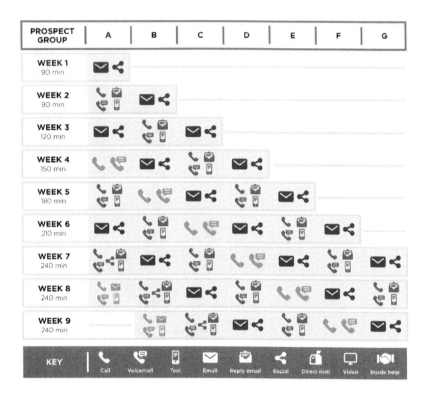

→   A — Finished (no activity)

→   B — Week 8 (their last week)

→   C — Week 7 (second-last week)

→   D — Week 6 of the cadence (3 weeks to go)

➜ E — Week 5 of the cadence (halfway through their cadence)

➜ F — Week 4 of the cadence (approaching the halfway point)

➜ G — Week 3 of the cadence (6 weeks left)

➜ H — Week 2 of the cadence (7 weeks to go)

➜ I — First attempts will be this week (email and light social touch)

With your A Group having reached the end of the cadence and your marketing requirements now fully behind you, you're looking at the same kind of prospecting workload as week 8. You've got a maximum of 40 prospects in your cadence and, once you factor in those who have dropped out or moved deeper into your pipeline, you're probably looking at around 2 hours and 30 minutes of prospecting time this week.

I've found that this system usually produces a reply rate of around 60 percent, so, in practice, this usually means two hours or so of prospecting (even when the cadence reaches its peak at week eight).

And so it continues. As you've probably noticed, the cadence doesn't really end after nine weeks. The nine weeks of the cadence are how long it takes us to introduce our 45 prospects and to ramp up our prospecting time so, including content, it's in the range of three to four hours per week.

Once we've reached the end of the nine weeks, we've got a lot of prospects in the cadence who've only received a few touches from us (Group I is only just getting to know us). We'll carry on with our prospecting, rolling each new prospect through at least eight weeks of outreach, using our first cadence as an outreach guideline.

Introduce new groups of prospects (five at a time) as space frees up in your cadence. Remember that message quality and consistency will beat quantity every time, so if you feel the urge to rush through your content preparation or (even worse) your outreach, you might have fed too many prospects into the system.

Remember that the nine-week cadence is only one possibility. You might find that a shorter or longer cadence is best for your organisation and your ideal clients. When you're building a custom cadence, simply map out your weekly touches and attempts and then, week by week, increase the prospects by a small amount every week, ensuring you load enough in to keep your pipeline strong and fresh, but not so many that you are overwhelmed. Remember that consistency is key. Never let valuable prospects slip through the cracks of your processes.

Don't Just Track—Adjust!

Sales messaging is fluid. Good sales reps adjust their outreach constantly. They combine persistence and flexibility, sticking to it long enough to get positive results whilst simultaneously making adjustments (small or large) when and as required. They sense changing prospect preferences as they happen and adjust their outreach accordingly.

Even if you are quite sure that you've found a cadence that fits your needs to a tee, remain flexible. What works today might not work tomorrow. What works tomorrow might not work in six months. Stay on your toes. Don't let the shifting market catch you flat-footed. Be on the lookout for any dips in outreach effectiveness (even small ones). If something stops working, run an A-B variation test. If your team is large enough, you can run multiple variations at a time, measuring effectiveness of new campaigns against your existing cadence.

When considering adjustments, be sure to look closely at each of the following:

➜ **Touch method:** Which method (phone, email or social) is working for you? Which one is providing lower level outcomes and could be replaced with another? Even if one method is underperforming, don't cut it out of your outreach entirely. Replace it with another channel. It's critical that your outreach moves in at least three (ideally four) channels.

➜ **Touch content:** How might your messaging be improved? How might the content that you send better capture your prospects' attention? How might content quality be improved? Is content the right length? Is it personalised enough? Are the CTAs clear and insistent?

➜ **Touch combination:** What combination of touches are producing the best results? Have you received any negative or positive feedback? How might a change of touch order affect your results?

➜   **Touch duration:** What duration is working well? If you've started with nine weeks, might a shorter cadence be enough? At what point are you seeing diminishing returns? To answer these questions, you'll need to test different cadence lengths. Every industry and buyer is different. The one-cadence-fits-all approach will usually result in your outreach being dismissed as spam.

The best reps make constant adjustments. They're not satisfied with *better* outcomes—they're constantly on the hunt for the *best* ones. Nothing else will do.

If you want to experiment with your cadence, run tests with batches of at least 25 prospects. Let's say you want to experiment with a new script. Run a 25-prospect cadence with the old script and another 25-prospect cadence with the new one. Which parts of the new script are getting positive responses? Which parts are falling flat? Measure your results and compare the two cadences (one new and one baseline) before you decide which cadence to carry forward.

Remember, change for change's sake is rarely a good idea. It confuses reps and can undo months of hard work in an instant. Make sure that adjustments in your cadence have been carefully considered and results have been properly measured.

Chapter 8
Social Selling

Making social a cornerstone of outreach is something I've been advocating for years. It's worked really well for me, generating a steady stream of consulting engagement for me and for my clients over the last five years. I've seen it help countless sellers supercharge their outreach. When your clients are active on LinkedIn, social outreach represents an excellent engagement opportunity. You can't afford to let this opportunity slip through your fingers.

There are three key reasons that everybody should make social selling a part of their outreach:

1. **It's brief** — Most reps prefer short and sweet communication. They like to cut straight to the point, and LinkedIn plays right into their hand. Powerful social engagements jump straight to the core of the exchange. Crafting a message takes seconds, and there's less pressure surrounding things like spelling and grammar (not my strong suit either).

2. **It's portable** — Using LinkedIn gives us access to our prospects on their mobile devices. One of the lasting souvenirs from my time in the military is impaired hearing. Thanks to hundreds of thousands of machine gun rounds, I lost 40 percent of hearing in my left ear and 30 percent in my right. Phone conversations are a constant struggle for me. I'd rather type than call. This doesn't put me at a disadvantage, though. People check their social messages far more often than they check their voicemails (more than emails too). It's a fast and nimble portable communication platform, and people *want* to use it.

3. **It's controllable** — Ethical persuasion and influence can be applied easily and more effectively through social media. With support from your social profiles and social content, you can create a construct for how you want prospects to see and perceive you.

A lot of reps have only a passing familiarity with LinkedIn and how it can be leveraged in outreach. In this chapter, I'll introduce you to a few social selling strategies that can make a world of difference in your outreach.

> **Optimise your profile for consistency.**
> **Even the best social strategy will fail if your profile and your outreach strategy and messaging are pulling in different directions.**

The Social Components

Social should play a strong supporting role in your cadence. Some reps have really leaned into social selling, doing all or the vast majority of their selling through social outreach. This may work for some, but I've found that this is too many eggs in too few baskets. The multi-channel approach I've advocated throughout this book will produce the best outcomes. How much time you spend in each channel is up to you. Even if you're strong on social, my advice is for you to go to other channels as well.

The role social plays in the cadence we looked at in the last chapter is a supporting one. There are examples and situations where you can use social as your primary outbound activity and do very well out of it as a business development tool. The cadence is designed to be adaptable. If your preferred mode of selling is social, you could easily tip the balance of the cadence towards more social outreach. I've provided a social cadence template in the appendices that assumes this kind of social-heavy approach.

When we look at social selling, we can see that there are a lot of moving parts. Each of them has its role to play in your outreach. In this section I'll spend a little time on each of them, starting with profile views.

Profile Views

Each visit to a person's profile generates a notification. When part of a multi-channel outreach, a simple profile view can be a great tool to use early in the cadence. Once prospects receive a notice you've viewed their profile they will often go to your profile and have a quick look around. This is a short-cut to a very early level of rapport and awareness. Later in the cadence, you can revisit your prospect's profile page to remind them that you're around and looking to chat.

If you receive a profile view in return, send them a short and casual message. Try something like, "Hey, I see we've crossed paths here in the last few days, I'm always happy to connect with more people in the XYZ industry. Would you be open to connecting?"

Likes

As on other platforms, LinkedIn offers you the chance to like a post in a number of ways. You can give them the classic thumbs up, an applause icon (celebrate), a lightbulb (insightful), a heart (I love it), or a purple face (curious). Whichever of these you choose, when you like a prospect's post, you're making a public statement of agreement.

Because of this, likes on LinkedIn are more valuable than likes on other platforms. LinkedIn activity does not tend to generate a high number of likes as a percentage of views, so we tend to notice when somebody has liked our post.

The simple act of liking your prospects' posts can really help build up small feelings of obligation, which you can then later leverage when you ask them to take some kind of action on your behalf. They might feel compelled to return the favour by liking some of your content. Often, you will know you have created a sense of obligation in the prospect or client if you see them responding in a similar fashion to your activity. Later, as the interaction builds, you can often use that sense of obligation as a lever to ask for a referral or some other activity.

If one of your prospects likes one of your posts, reach out and strike whilst the iron is hot. This is an ideal opportunity to start a productive conversation. Try something like the following:

"Hey Gary, I see you liked my post on sales skills. Thanks for the interaction, much appreciated. You know, if you liked that, you might also like this piece I found from Dean on how to motivate sales reps. Hope you like it."

When these messages are delivered in the right way and at the right time, the prospect is often grateful and therefore open to meaningful conversations. If you have a fear of outbound, social outreach like this can be a powerful and easy strategy to employ.

Comments

Comments drive outcomes in ways similar to likes, but they are even more valuable—provided that we engage in a meaningful way with the prospect's post or content. Commenting "Nice post" or "Great stuff" won't be nearly as effective as asking a detailed question or sharing an insight that connects directly to their post.

You can also tag prospects in posts (either your own or somebody else's), but only if you are quite certain that they'll find the post extremely interesting or at least useful. Remember, by doing this, you're asking them to commit to reading or to responding, so you best not be too flippant about the requests. Too many of these and you'll simply be ignored. To tag or mention somebody in a post, use the @ symbol before their name.

Tags or mentions are also a good opportunity to highlight a shared connection. On one of your prospect's posts, tag or mention a common connection in a comment. The conversations that result often open doors.

Shares

Sharing somebody's post with your network is the highest compliment you can pay to somebody on LinkedIn. Even still, there are levels to this. If you simply hit the share button, you haven't done much more than hitting the like button. Best practice is to include a comment introducing whatever you're sharing to your connections and why you think it's valuable. Tag the original poster in this comment and perhaps a few others to start a conversation.

When you use their content to drive engagement, you're creating strong alignment between yourself and the prospect.

Articles

Finding an article and sharing it or distributing it on social is a great way to support ongoing conversations with your prospects. What works really well is if the content is from a third party, specifically someone with a recognised level of authority (e.g., an industry veteran or a celebrity).

Sharing articles allows us to interrupt our prospects, telling them, "Hey, it's not just me. Look what these thought leaders are saying about this." You're showing them that the path forward you're proposing is supported by experts. Do this right and they'll want to talk to you.

There are several ways we can use articles in a social context. We can send the article directly to them via a messaging service such as InMail or LinkedIn message; we can post the article and mention or tag them in the post or in a comment; or we can find the article posted somewhere and simply tag them inside the comment section and make a short supporting message—something like this: "Hey Gary, we were talking about this last week — thought this might be of interest." All of these work well. Use identical strategies when sharing your own articles, your company's marketing material, or third-party articles.

I've always found it helpful to keep a folder of articles in my OneNote that other prospects have found interesting. I organise the articles in sub-folders so I can find a relevant piece of content and distribute it quickly and easily. Having my content organised like this means I can take action very quickly and not get bogged down trying to find the right piece.

InMail versus Messaging

InMails are typically what you would use to reach out to people before you have connected with them. This form of outreach has been overused by spammers and sponsored outreach, so it's not the most potent form of interaction. The well hasn't run entirely dry, though. It's still well worth a try.

Keep things brief. Think of InMails as an abbreviated email. In most cases, they will pop up in your prospect's inbox as an email from LinkedIn, which it about as useful as an email. Lots of people link their LinkedIn account to their private email, so this provides us with reason to be both cautious and optimistic.

We should be a cautious because people may see your professional outreach as an unwanted intrusion in their 'personal' email inbox. If your message is truly customer centric, you'll circumnavigate this more easily. We should be optimistic because if we've emailed them at work and we've sent them an InMail, we are multi-threading them on the one channel, potentially across multiple addresses. We're popping up in multiple inboxes, increasing the chances they'll see at least one of our messages. When you don't have access to many channels, this is a nice way to increase your channel count.

Once we've connected with the prospect, we can message them directly through the platform, and I've found this to be a powerful form of outreach—especially when combined with the persuasion techniques we discussed earlier. Message notifications often go directly to their mobile devices, so our outreach is getting through to them wherever they are. To take full advantage of this, keep it brief. Messages should be a cross between a very short email and a text message.

The 7 Secrets of Social Selling

We'll close this chapter with my framework for social selling success. The infographic above has been my go-to framework since 2014, and it continues to be a highly reliable platform to drive excellent social selling results.

Secret #1 — Build a Compelling Profile

Key Strategy: Your profile must be so compelling that when one of your ideal clients sees your profile, they should think,

That's someone I want to have in my network. They either send you a connection request or they accept yours.

Creating a compelling profile is the most critical part of your LinkedIn strategy. So much of what happens on LinkedIn happens only after prospects have first looked at your profile. You want prospects who visit your profile to feel compelled to connect.

Three quarters of B2B buyers will do some form of research before they buy. They'll be looking not only at the business you work for but also at you as part of their buying process. Most of them will go straight to LinkedIn. The rest will Google you which will almost certainly bring them straight to your LinkedIn page. Like it or not, whether you're an embracer of digital communication or not, your buyers are visiting your LinkedIn profile. It has to support your sales activities, not diminish them.

➡ Profile picture — Head and shoulders only. You should be wearing professional attire. No pets, partners, sunglasses, logos or sporting attire (unless these are clearly connected to your brand).

➡ Background image — This should support your image and your messages. A call to action can be really effec- tive. A corporate image from marketing can work as well. A popular choice is a geographically specific picture. For example, if you're based in San Francisco, a picture of the Golden Gate Bridge immediately tells visitors to your page where you're doing business.

➡ Headline — Explain how you help people, who you help,

and where. Your title is in your experience section, so you don't need to include it in your headline. The exception would be if you have a very senior role at a medium to large organisation and that title carries significant authority of its own (e.g., Chief Sales Officer, Salesforce Inc.).

→ Summary — Similar to your headline, only a little more in-depth. Use your summary to provide a touch more detail about how you help people and what kind of people you help. Don't use this space to sing your own praises or summarise your employment history. Instead talk about what you do and how people can get in touch with you.

→ Experience — Make sure you link your account with your organisation's or your employer's LinkedIn account (their business page). This link means when someone searches that business name, they will find you associated with that corporation. This link is important because it's highly likely people will remember who you work for and, perhaps, your first name. They will then go to your employer's page to find you. For example, if I was speaking to James from JP Morgan in Sydney but could not recall his last name, by going to JP Morgan's LinkedIn page and searching for his name, I should be able to track him down.

→ NB: Your profile should not look like a CV or resume. That was what LinkedIn was for all those years ago. It's changed.

The good news is that your profile doesn't need to be 100 percent filled in. It's the key areas that I've covered above that matter most. Heat maps show us that people only spend a small portion of time on key areas of your profile. Most visitors look at your picture, background, headline, summary and experience. The other areas are important but these five are the non-negotiables.

Secret #2: Build a Professional Network

Key Strategy: Not everyone is your ideal client. Connecting with everyone will ruin your LinkedIn feed.

The quality of your feed determines your effectiveness on social. The quality of your feed is determined by the quality of the connections you have and the people you follow.

There are many social media platforms, and the conversation is different across each of them. LinkedIn is predominantly a professional platform. Therefore, being connected to friends, family and people from faraway places where you will not and cannot do business will reduce your effectiveness on LinkedIn.

Have a clear description of your ideal client(s) and deliberately build out a network, profile, and content strategy that they will find compelling and interesting.

Secret #3: Connect with Confidence

Key Strategy: Having a strong base of connections who are similar is valuable to both you and to others who are in that network with you. Ask for a connection if there is alignment, and say why you think the connection makes sense for *both of you.*

If you've followed Secret #2 and built a highly profession-al profile and network, you should be able to connect with confidence. The alignment between you and your prospects should be clear, and it should seem like a natural choice for them to agree to your request to connect. They might even wonder why they haven't connected with you already.

When sending connection requests, always customise them. Never send a blank connection request. You want to encour-age people to use this chance to communicate and to show them that there's a very good reason to connect and it's in their benefit. You're not trying to sneak in the back door. You're announcing yourself at the front gate.

Use a persuasion or influence strategy in your connec-tion request to increase the chances of getting a *yes* and decrease the chances of getting a *no.* A simple liking strat-egy (paying them a genuine compliment or highlighting things or connections you share in common) will increase your connection rates significantly.

If you want to connect with confidence and grow your valu-able network, this is the best piece of tactical advice I can give you. Adopt a viewing strategy. This starts with a search for your ideal clients using SalesNAV or regular LinkedIn. Drill down to find your perfect clients by company size, title, location, and second connection. If you are in SalesNAV, you can make the search even narrower by clicking on 'Posted on LinkedIn in the last 30 days'. This should help you avoid those who are not active on the platform.

You should have a rather large list of profiles. Visit 50 profiles every day. When you make your approach strategic like this, you'll notice that you get a bunch of people looking back at your profile every day. You'll also get a number of connection requests—many of these from people you've already selected as ideal potential clients. Each of these connection requests represents an unparalleled opportunity to strike up a meaningful conversation.

A more advanced version of this strategy is to follow this up a few days after your profile viewing spree. There will be a list of people who viewed your profile but didn't send you a connection request. Reach out to them by asking them to connect and include a personalised message. Something like this is often effective:

"Hey Mary, I see we've crossed paths here in the last few days, and I'm always happy to have more Sydney-based sales directors in the network.

Hope you agree,

Mark Mc."

This strategy is persuasive because they've looked at your profile (and now they know that you know that). The persuasion principle of consistency comes into play. More likely than not, they'll accept your connection request. They're certainly much less likely to report you to LinkedIn as someone "I don't know".

Secret #4: Have an Engagement Strategy

Key Strategy: It's all well and good having lots of connections on LinkedIn. However, we need to take it further and have something we can share that will help us start valuable conversations about what we do or, if it can't do this, at least leave a positive impression.

Keep content on hand to send to new connections. Show them immediately that you are not just farming for likes and connections. Start with an engagement strategy. This might mean hosting a rolling event like a meetup or a lunch and learn every 12 weeks. When you connect, invite your new connections to your next event. If hosting an event is impractical, have some content to share—perhaps something eye-catching like an infographic, e-book, or white paper.

Very few people open relationships on social with a gift. This sets you apart from everyone else and is a nice reciprocity play. If you have given something that is unexpected, perceived as valuable, timely, and personalised, there is an increased sense of obligation on behalf of the receiver—perhaps enough to start a conversation.

Secret #5 Leverage Your Existing Connections

Key Strategy: Once they've connected with someone and swapped their first message, many people forget about these new connections and move on, focusing their time on connecting with more people rather than on building a relationship with their existing connections. To turn a shallow engagement into a meaningful one, spend time deepening connections rather than moving on to the next target.

This doesn't have to mean naming your first-born in their honour. You've just got to keep the relationship active. Set aside time to like and comment on your connections' posts from time to time. This activity builds a feeling of obligation or reciprocation that you can use as a lever to get a meeting or a referral or just to start a conversation.

For prospects who are deeper in your pipeline, a professional recommendation can be a powerful way to deepen the relationship (spelling and grammar are important here as these will appear on their profile). The icing on the cake: they'll often send you a professional recommendation in return. It's reciprocity at work!

Look for opportunities to connect your connections with others on the platform. Being valuable and visible is a great way to stay top of mind and be seen as a worthwhile connection.

Secret #6 Consistency & Discipline

Key Strategy: All social media has a scrolling feed, a timeline. Being consistent and disciplined is the best approach to managing your social interactions.

Like other aspects of prospecting, three or four small investments of time will pay much bigger dividends than trying to do it all in one go. Bunching your LinkedIn activity and efforts into just one block per week will mean you get buried at the bottom of your prospects' feeds. You'll also miss many of your ideal clients' posts and comments. Social works in a timely manner; most activity takes place 24 to 48 hours after the original post.

The best time to start conversations is when your prospects are online. Many of these are outside normal office hours, but you'll find the investment of 15 minutes here and there in these slots will pay dividends. These are the times that I've found to be the best for social outreach:

➜ Monday: 18:30 — 21:00

➜ Tuesday: 08:00 — 09:00 and 18:30 — 21:00

➜ Wednesday: 08:00 — 09:00 and 16:30 — 21:00

➜ Thursday: 08:00 — 09:00

➜ Friday and Saturday: Ineffective

➜ Sunday: 14:00 — 17:00

Secret #7 Convert Social Activity into Sales Activity

Key Strategy: Don't make the mistake of getting too caught up in the number of likes, connections, and comments you get from your activity. These are simply vanity metrics and not the measure of social success.

The activities that LinkedIn is trying to guide you towards might not actually be in your best interest as a rep. Adding endless connections is a good example.

Once someone likes or comments on one of your posts or articles, take the time to follow up, either via LinkedIn message, by email, or you can always pick up the phone. I like to treat social activity like an old-school inbound phone call or general enquiry. Take the opportunity to ask if you can help them and provide a deeper level of interaction.

Social interaction in this context is designed to support your new business activities.

* * *

Remember that, no matter how persuasive your connection request, InMail, or social message, there are some prospects who will not interact with you. Some will simply ignore requests, but, far more often, it's because they are not truly active on LinkedIn. They might have an account, but it may have been months or longer since they last checked it.

Only half of those who have LinkedIn accounts check them regularly. Even fewer are active users. To get an indication of this, check their activity. If they have liked, shared or commented recently, you're in luck. If their profile looks out of date, or if it looks like a CV and they are talking about how they are a great team leader (or any other dated language) chances are pursuing them via LinkedIn will not be successful.

Social selling has been a strong focus area for me for the

last five years, so you can find a lot of content on this topic on both my LinkedIn page and on my YouTube channel. My advice is constantly adapting to the latest findings and trends. I invite you to follow me for up-to-date social selling strategies.

Conclusion

I want to leave you with one final piece of advice, and it brings us full circle. Very early in this book, I told you that the right mindset is key to prospecting success. All sales take place above the neck.

A big part of the right mindset is the ability to clear away the distractions and bring our full attention to every engagement. This is easier said than done when you're taking an entirely new approach to your outreach.

We've covered a lot of ground in this book. You're looking down the barrel at a period of change and adjustment. There are new strategies to apply and new routines to adapt. You'll slide into some of these routines like an old pair of marching boots. Others will take some time to break in.

It might feel like you've got a brainful, but everything will fall to place when you start putting the strategies we've covered in this book into practice. The cadence—when properly and diligently applied—clears away mental clutter (especially the doubts and insecurities that make outreach selling seem more difficult than it actually is).

The key to all this is to remember that prospecting with a cadence isn't complex. It's actually quite the opposite. It gets easier each time you roll through a new cadence. There will be an adjustment period, but after that time has passed, you'll find it impossible to imagine doing your outreach any other way.

To make getting from here to there easier, I want to close by highlighting some of this book's key takeaways. Even if you remember nothing else from this book, these key points will help you become a more effective sales rep.

The 10 Key Takeaways

#1: Consistently Good Beats Occasionally Great
Rather than focusing on that big win, focus on a steady, day-in-day-out approach that will produce results.

#2: Hit Them Between the Eyes
For truly effective outreach, put the work in to understand your customers and their unique problems. The tighter your focus, the better.

#3: Use the Powerful Principles of Persuasion
To give your outreach a powerful boost, use the principles of persuasion, but make sure that your persuasion is always honest and ethical.

#4: Focus on Your Client's Outcomes—Not Your Own
The most successful reps keep their eye trained on their prospects' problems, not their own. Everything should be about the commercial outcomes your clients can expect.

#5: Prepare for Success
Preparation makes all the difference. Spend time each week preparing scripts and content for next week's outreach. Don't risk flying by the seat of your pants.

#6: Spread Your Outreach into Multiple Channels
The best outreach strategies touch prospects in at least three or four different channels.

#7: Make it Rapid-Fire
When spreading your outreach across multiple channels, build a sense of urgency by sending all your messages in a narrow window (ideally around two minutes).

#8: Beware of Sellers' Bias
Stop thinking of your outreach as a nuisance. Start seeing yourself as a valuable partner. You aren't a problem. You're the solution.

#9: Feed Prospects into the Pipeline Gradually
Focus on quality over quantity. This means adding prospects slowly (ideally in groups of five).

#10: Embrace Social
Using LinkedIn as a platform for your outreach will dramatically improve the effectiveness of that outreach. Approach social selling with a strategic plan and engagement strategy.

Acknowledgements

Getting this book into your hands was not something I could have done entirely on my own. There are several people who deserve a special mention and recognition for their significant contributions.

Dean Mannix is a master sales trainer, motivator, and speaker, and he has been a mentor for several years. For more than half a decade now, I've been proud to call him a very good friend. Dean is an expert in breaking down sales strategies in ways that are accessible and effective, and he has inspired me in so many ways that his strategies are scattered throughout this book, either in slightly modified form or (in a few places) in his exact words. Without Dean's support and teachings, what you hold in your hands would be little more than an A4 pamphlet. Thank you Dean and Terresa for your friendship and tireless generosity.

Jack Daly was the first person who made me understand that sales could be viewed as a set of systems and processes—not some dark art. The first time I saw Jack, in the early 2000s, he left me wide eyed and keen to learn more about sales psychology and the sales training space. Since then, he's been a constant source of insight and inspiration. I knew I wanted to learn all about those systems and processes as quickly as I could. Jack, like Dean, provides sales reps and sales leaders with super practical sales strategies for sellers to follow. Jack is also ex-Military and has the most incredible drive and discipline I have ever seen. Jack, thanks for the endless motivation.

To Chantelle, my wife, and Davis, our loyal Staffy cross. Thanks for the continued support and for the freedom to choose my own path. Wherever that might lead us.

To Bryan Szabo, my editor: without his guidance and assistance this would still be scraps of poorly assembled notes. Thank you for guiding me through this incredible process. If you are reading this and thinking about writing a book of your own, I encourage you to reach out to Bryan through LinkedIn.

I want to single out a few other people whose content, training, books, videos and resources have helped shape my thoughts on the sales space and are partly reproduced here: Phil M Jones, Tony J Hughes, John Barrows, Cian Mcloughlin, John Dougan, Brian Tracy, Zig Ziglar, Dr Robert Cialdini, Jeb Blount, Anthony Iannarino, Dale Carnegie, Chris Voss, Jim Rohan, and Graham Hawkins.

Appendix 1

Cadence Rhythms

Standard 8 Week Cadence

Social Cadence Example

Longer Cadence With Week Off

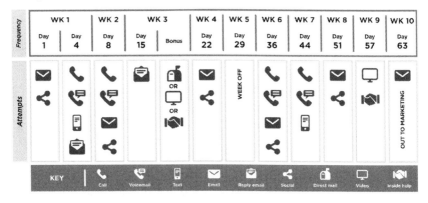

Enterprise/Government Cadence

B2B Professional 4 Week Cadence

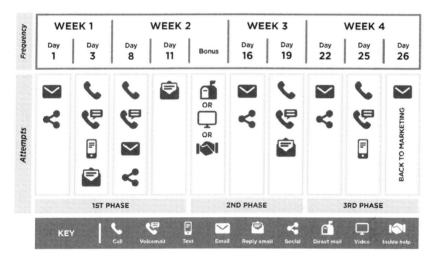

Appendix 2
Ideal Client Profile

Company Data

Location:

Industry:

Company Employees (#):

Turn Over PA:

What are their 3 primary business challenges or priorities right now?

1) _____

2) _____

3) _____

4) _____

What business events might create a buying window (e.g., increased/decreased staff numbers, M&A activity, fundraising, new location, new senior executive staff, etc.)?

_____

_____

_____

_____

Persona Data

Age range: 20-30 / 30-40 / 40-50 / 50-60 / 60+

Gender: M / F / Unimportant

Presumed education level: Secondary / Some post-secondary / Technical College / Bachelor's Degree / Master's / Doctorate

Do they make decisions fast or slow?

_____

What can you say about their personality? Do they typically fit a particular type?

_____

What is their preferred communication channel? What is their second favourite?

_____

Do they spend their day behind a desk, or are they on the move all day?

_____

Are they more likely to answer their desk phone or their mobile?

_____

How do they receive internal communications? Email? Text? Phone call?

_____

Are they active on social media? If so, which platforms do they probably use?

_____

In what channels are other reps/suppliers trying to reach them?

_____

Content Strategy:

What key insights do I have that might help them solve their business challenges or achieve their priorities?

_____

How can I demonstrate that I have experience solving their particular problems?

_____

What content do I have on hand/what content can I create that will serve as an agitation piece or conversation starter?

_____

What will be the most effective way of delivering this content?

_____

Appendix 3
Scripts

Before we begin looking at some of the resources and templates I've included in this appendix, I'd like to direct you to my website, where you'll find an Excel Planner and my Cadence Template, both of which will serve as the foundation of the cadence you'll build with the help of the materials in this section of the book.

You can find these resources on my website:
www.markmc.co/tpg

Below, you'll find all the scripts we discussed in the week-by-week cadence breakdown chapter. We'll be making one attempt per week, with multiple touches per attempt. You can scale this up or down depending on your particular needs or replace the touches with those you think will be more valuable to your prospects.

Remember that this is just baseline content. Make adjustments as required—especially whenever outcomes are less than hoped for.

Here's what you'll find in this section:

2 x Phone scripts
>1 x Introduction
>1 x Public signal

2 x Voicemail scripts
>1 x Basic
>1 x Close-out

2 x Text scripts
>1 x Here are my details
>1 x Outbound

3 x Email scripts
>1 x Super cold introduction (template and completed)
>1 x Public signal introduction (template and completed)
>1 x Content email (template and completed)

2 x Reply email scripts
>1 x Introduction (template and completed)
>1 x Reply email (template and completed)

2 x LinkedIn connection scripts
>1 x Request option 1
>1 x Request option 2

5 x LinkedIn scripts
>1 x Post connection script
>2 x Share article script
>2 x Ask scripts (direct and softer)

Phone Script 1 — Quick Introduction

*Hey **PROSPECT'S NAME**, thanks for taking my call, do you have a moment?*

Wait for positive response

*OK, this is **YOUR NAME AND ORGANISATION**. The reason for my call today is we've been working with **TARGET GROUP**[1] to help them with **BUSINESS PROBLEM**,[2] and I was wondering what's the best way for us to get some time in your diary to share some details with you?*

Wait for permission to proceed

I appreciate that you weren't expecting my call, so I'll be brief.

If they're busy, simply book a convenient time for you to call back

---

1   Example: Sales directors of tech businesses
2   Example: Developing team prospecting and selling skills

Phone Script 2 — Public Signal

Hi **PROSPECT'S NAME**, *this is* **YOUR NAME** *from* **ORGANISATION***.*

I recently noticed your **PUBLIC SIGNAL,**[3] *and I thought we should talk. Do you have a moment?*

When I saw your **PUBLIC SIGNAL***, I realised that we had completed some* **PROJECT**[4] *for a very similar organisation,* **CLIENT***.*

Working with **CLIENT** *and others like them, we have developed some really valuable insights to share with* **ROLE**[5] *like yourself that might change your approach going forward.*

What's the best way for us to get some time in your diary to share those details?

---

3   Examples: A new billboard, a company vehicle, or a construction site
4   Examples: Fleet analysis, sales effectiveness analysis, etc.
5   Examples: Fleet managers, sales managers, etc.

Voicemail Script 1 — Basic

Hey PROSPECT'S NAME,

You should now have an important executive briefing in your email that I believe will be very insightful for you. I'm calling to try to organise a time to share some of the deeper, more granular detail with you.

*It's **YOUR NAME** from **ABC Fleet**, I'll try to connect with you again soon **(OR)** in the next **XXX** days.*

Voicemail Script 2 — Close-Out

Hey **PROSPECT'S NAME,**

*I've been unsuccessful in reaching you to date, but based on what we know from working with other **XXXX's,** I'm confident that there are some very compelling reasons for both you and your organisation to be having a chat with us about this.*

*If you get this in the next few days, drop me a call. Otherwise, what I'm going to do is **ACTION.**[6]*

*It's **YOUR NAME** from **ORGANISATION.** I'm on **NUMBER.***

---

6   Examples: Call in six months, add them to the marketing funnel, place them in your CRM, etc.

Text Script 1 — Here Are My Details

PROSPECT'S NAME, YOUR NAME *from* ***ORGANISATION****. Completely understand you not picking up an unknown number. Here are my details.*

ATTACH AN ELECTRONIC BUSINESS CARD/SHARE CONTACT INFORMATION

I'll be reaching out again in the next few days. Looking forward to chatting.

Text Script 2 — Outbound Text

PROSPECT'S NAME, YOUR NAME *from* **ORANISATION.** *Just connecting regarding helping with* **BUSINESS BENEFIT.**[7] *I will get in touch later in the week/next week.*

---

7   Examples: Optimising your fleet, increasing your sales team's effectiveness, etc.

Email Script 1 — Super Cold Introduction

PROSPECT'S NAME,

*We talk to **TITLE AND INDUSTRY** every week; many tell us their team is struggling with the following:*

- *BUSINESS CHALLENGE #1*
- *BUSINESS CHALLENGE #2*
- *BUSINESS CHALLENGE #3*

*Is this consistent with what you're seeing at **PROSPECT'S ORGANISATION**, or **UNLIKELY POSITIVE SCENARIO**?*

*Having worked with others in the **INDUSTRY** space (**CLIENT EXAMPLES**) there is a bunch of experience we can share on how they've been able to **BUSINESS BENEFIT**.*

***PROSPECT'S NAME**, I'll give you a call in the next three days to see if we can discuss this in more detail.*

YOUR NAME
TITLE

Email Script 1 — Super Cold Introduction (completed example)

Gavin,

We talk to Sales Directors of Tech companies every week; many tell us their team is struggling with the following:

- *Finding new clients*
- *Starting meaningful conversations that turn into opportunities*
- *Moving their approach from transactional into a more strategic 'trusted advisor' style of sale*

Is this consistent with what you're seeing at B.I.G. Tech, or is the large majority of your team hitting their quotas monthly?

Having worked with others in the tech space (Datto, Dim Data, Fortinet, etc.), there is a bunch of experience we can share on how they've been able to close this gap in a repeatable and sustainable way.

Gavin, I'll give you a call in the next three days to see if we can discuss this in more detail.

Mark McInnes
Mark Mc — Sales Training

Email Script 2 — Public Signal Introduction

Hi **PROSPECT'S NAME,**

*I noticed your **PUBLIC SIGNAL** and it reminded me that we recently completed **PROJECT** for another **INDUSTRY** organisation.*

*We have some strong insights available around **TOPIC** in the format of a short executive briefing. I think you'll find the detail as interesting as they did.*

I will reach out to confirm a suitable time in the next few days.

Looking forward to chatting.

YOUR NAME

Email Script 2 — Public Signal Introduction (completed example)

Hi Kevin,

I noticed one of your delivery trucks parked outside the Smith Shop in North Sydney on Tuesday, and it reminded me that we recently completed some vehicle tracking work for another produce delivery organisation.

We have some strong insights available around how vehicle tracking reduces delivery delays for other early-morning delivery companies in the format of a short executive briefing. I think you'll find the detail as interesting as they did.

I will reach out to confirm a suitable time in the next few days.

Looking forward to chatting.

Mark Mc

Email Script 3 — Content Email

Hi **PROSPECT'S NAME,**

SOURCE just ran an article by **AUTHOR** that covers **RELEVANT TOPIC.**

I've attached it here for you. Go straight to **LOCATION IN CONTENT** for the relevant detail.

Why I thought it would interest you specifically is **CONNECT ARTICLE TO BUSINESS PROBLEM.**

I would be interested to hear how you are preparing for these challenges.

I'll drop you a call next week to see if we can have a short discussion.

Best,

YOUR NAME

Email Script 3 — Content Email (completed example)

Hi Tim,

Forbes magazine has just run an article by Steven Covey (a motivational/social psychology expert) that covers the impact demotivated sales teams can have on organisations.

I've attached it here for you. Go straight to page 9 for the relevant detail.

Why I thought it would interest you specifically is that Covey uses tech organisations just like yours as his example.

I would be interested to hear how you are preparing for these challenges.

I'll drop you a call next week to see if we can have a short discussion.

Best,

Mark Mc

Email Script 4 — Close-Out

PROSPECT'S NAME,

It's a shame we did not get an opportunity to discuss **TOPIC.** *I understand people often have other, more pressing priorities.*

I still believe, because of the experience we have in **INDUSTRY,** *that a discussion around this would be well worth your time.*

PROSPECT'S NAME, *if you'd like to discuss* **TOPIC** *in the future, I hope you'll feel comfortable reaching out to us here.*

What I'm going to do is reach out again in **TIMEFRAME.**

Yours professionally,

YOUR NAME

Reply Email Script 1 — Introduction

*Hi **INSERT NAME***

Very keen to coordinate a conversation about ***INSIGHT***.

As an example, one of our clients, ***CLIENT NAME***, who also ***SIMILARITY***, was able to use the ***INSIGHT*** to ***BUSINESS BENEFITS***.

Would any of these be a focus for you and ***THEIR BUSINESS NAME***, or would you use ***INSIGHT*** to help in another way?

What day would best suit you in the next ***TIMEFRAME***?

Looking forward to connecting.

YOUR NAME

Reply Email Script 1 — Introduction (completed example)

Hi Karen,

Very keen to coordinate a conversation about the fleet efficiency insights now available to you.

As an example, one of our clients, Speedway Delivery, who also have 15 cars, was able to use the deeper detail I shared to save $450 per car over the course of a year. As a result, they were able to employ more sales resources and reduce their fleet size by 8 percent.

Would any of these be a focus for you and FlimFlam, or would you use extra fleet capacity to help in another way?

What day would best suit you in the next three weeks?

Looking forward to connecting.

Craig.

Reply Email Script 2 — Reply Email

Hi **PROSPECT'S NAME,**

What did you think of the **CONTENT TYPE**?-

The most relevant piece for you was **RELEVANT DETAIL**.

INSERT 2-3 SENTENCES DESCRIBING DETAIL

INSERT 1 SENTENCE DESCRIBING BENEFIT GAINED/ RISK AVOIDED

I am planning on being in **LOCATION** next week to meet with another client and would be happy to catch up with you also.

Is it a ridiculous idea to try and find a time on **DAY**?

Best,

YOUR NAME

Reply Email Script 2 — Reply Email (completed example)

Hi Carl,

What did you think of the video?-

The most relevant piece for you was the way the vehicles were able to be tracked after they've been to the early morning market.

That business has been able to make sure all their customers get their deliveries on time and they can advise the stores when to expect deliveries much more accurately. This means fewer customer complaints and much more transparency for the management team.

You'll be able to see things going wrong well before they impact your business.

I am planning on being in Melbourne next week to meet with another client and would be happy to catch up with you also.

Is it a ridiculous idea to try and find a time on Thursday?

Best,
Mark Mc

LinkedIn Connection Request Script 1

PROSPECT'S NAME,

Hoping we can connect as I share regular content designed to help **PROFESSION AND BENEFIT.**[8]

It made sense to extend my outreach to you by connecting on LinkedIn.

Hope you agree.

Best,

YOUR NAME

---

8   Example: I regularly share content designed to help fleet professionals make better day-to-day decisions.

LinkedIn Connection Request Script 2

PROSPECT'S NAME,

Because you also have a focus on **PRODUCT/SERVICE FOCUS,**[9] *it just made sense to reach out for a connection. I promise to regularly share valuable content around our industry if you agree to connect.*

Best,

YOUR NAME

---

9   Example: Because you also have a focus on fleet operations...

LinkedIn Post Connection Message 1

PROSPECT'S NAME,

*Great to have another **PROFESSION** in the network. I'm pretty active here on **LinkedIn/Twitter.** I hope you enjoy the interaction.*
*Here is a **XXXX** as a connection gift — welcome aboard.*

Looking forward to seeing you around the platform.

Best,

YOUR NAME

LinkedIn Share Article Script 1

PROSPECT'S NAME,

*I noticed you liked that article on **ARTICLE TOPIC/ NAME**. Because you liked that, I thought you might like this one too. **ARTICLE NAME OR AUTHOR** also references **TOPIC**. The main points are easy to find if you go straight to **LOCATION**.*

Looking forward to seeing you around the platform.

Best,

YOUR NAME

LinkedIn Share Article Script 2

I noticed you liked that article on **TOPIC**. *Because you liked that article, I thought you might like this one too.*

PROSPECT'S NAME, *I would be interested in your take on what you think this means for* ***TOPIC/INDUSTRY.***

Best,

YOUR NAME

LinkedIn Ask Script 1 (Direct)

Really appreciate the interaction here, **PROSPECT'S NAME**. *It all helps the 'social world' go around and stay active. We clearly have a number of similar interests on here. Would you be open to grabbing a* **VC/ CHAT/MEETING** *sometime in the next few weeks?*

Either way, catch you on the platform soon.

YOUR NAME

LinkedIn Ask Script 2 (Softer)

Hey **PROSPECT'S NAME,**

I've been reaching out to my current clients to invite them to this **WEBINAR/EVENT/LIVE STREAM** on **TOPIC**. I thought it made sense to invite you too.

Provide details

Because you're in **INDUSTRY/LOCATION/ROLE** this might be valuable to you because **REASON.**

Either way, catch you on the platform soon.

YOUR NAME

About the Author

Mark is a highly regarded sales professional who draws heavily on his time in the Australian Army as an Assault Trooper, where amongst other things, he worked alongside the Queens Guards at Windsor Castle, London.

As a sales trainer to APAC's business sector, Mark's strong focus on the top of the sales funnel helps his clients find and engage with more customers in a credible and ethical way. Ranked the #1 Australian Social Seller on LinkedIn by LinkedIn, Mark has the ability to combine digital selling techniques with traditional sales strategies. Sectors that Mark typically works with include FMCG, Tech, SaaS, Fin-Tech, Fin-Services, Education, Business Services and Hospitality.

If you're a front-line rep, a sales leader or enabler, reach out to Mark on LinkedIn to start a prospecting discussion. For access to updated outreach scripts, templates and strategies go to **www.markmc.co/tpg** and subscribe.

Printed in Great Britain
by Amazon

19529359R00109